GROWING OLD, FINISHING STRONG

GROWING OLD, FINISHING STRONG

How to Make the Most of the Years You've Got Left

SANFORD ZENSEN

WIPF & STOCK · Eugene, Oregon

GROWING OLD, FINISHING STRONG
How to Make the Most of the Years You've Got Left

Copyright © 2025 Sanford Zensen.

All rights reserved. Except for brief quotations in critical publications or reviews, no part of this book may be reproduced in any manner without prior written permission from the publisher.

Write: Permissions, Wipf and Stock Publishers, 199 W. 8th Ave., Suite 3, Eugene, OR 97401

Wipf & Stock
An imprint of Wipf & Stock Publishers

199 W. 8th Ave., Suite # 3
Eugene, OR 97401
www.wipfandstock.com

PAPERBACK ISBN: 979-8-3852-5826-0

HARDCOVER ISBN: 979-8-3852-5827-7

EBOOK ISBN: 979-8-3852-5828-4

Unless otherwise noted Scripture quotations are taken from the *New American Standard Bible*® (NASB), Copyright © 1960, 1962, 1963, 1968, 1971, 1972, 1973,1975, 1977, 1995 by The Lockman Foundation. Used by permission. www.Lockman.org.

Scripture quotations marked (ASV are taken from the *American Standard Version* (1901), Public Domain.

Scripture quotations marked (AMP) are taken from the *Amplified® Bible*, Copyright © 2015 by The Lockman Foundation. Used by permission. www.Lockman.org.

Scripture quotations marked (AMPC) are taken from the *Amplified Bible, Classic Education,* Copyright © 1965 2015 by The Lockman Foundation. Used by permission. www.Lockman.org.

Scripture quotations marked (ESV) are from *The Holy Bible, English Standard Version*® (ESV®), copyright © 2001 by Crossway, a publishing ministry of Good News Publishers. Used by permission. All rights reserved.

Scriptures marked (KJV) are taken from the *King James Version*, public domain.

Scripture quotations marked (MSG) are taken from *The Message*, copyright © 1993, 1994, 1995, 1996, 2000, 2001, 2002 by Eugene H. Peterson. Used by permission of NavPress. All rights reserved. Represented by Tyndale House Publishers, Inc.

Scripture marked (NKJV) taken from the *New King James Version*®. Copyright © 1982 by Thomas Nelson. Used by permission.

Scripture quotations marked (NIV) are taken from the Holy Bible, *New International Version*®, NIV®. Copyright © 1973, 1978, 1984, 2011 by Biblica, Inc.™ Used by permission of Zondervan. All rights reserved worldwide. www.zondervan.com The "NIV" and "New International Version" are trademarks registered in the United States Patent and Trademark Office by Biblica, Inc.™

Scripture quotations marked (NLT) are taken from the Holy Bible, *New Living Translation* Copyright © 1996, 2004, 2007 by Tyndale House Foundation. Used by permission of Tyndale House Publishers Inc., Carol Stream, IL 60188. All rights reserved. New Living, NLT, and the New Living Translation logo are registered trademarks of Tyndale House Publishers.

Scripture quotations marked (PHILLIPS) are taken from *The New Testament in Modern English*, copyright 1958, 1959, 1960 J.B. Phillips and 1947, 1952, 1955, 1957, 1976, The MacMillan Company, New York. Used by permission. All rights reserved.

Scripture quotations marked (TPT) are from *The Passion Translation*®. Copyright © 2017, 2018 by Passion & Fire Ministries, Inc. Used by permission. All rights reserved. ThePassionTranslation.com.

Scripture quotations marked (ASV) are taken from *American Standard Version*, Public domain.

Bracketed ( ) comments in Scripture and quotes are the author's.

"My prayer is that when I die, all hell rejoices that I am out of the fight."[1]

–C.S. Lewis

---

[1] C.S, Lewis, *Informal Institute for National Security Thinkers and Practitioners, Quotes of the Day* No date, retrieved from https://myemail.constantcontact.com/9-3-24-National-Security-News-and-Commentary.html?soid=1114009586911&aid=CMS4iMTcTDA

Dedication

For Sharon, who has walked with me through life for nearly sixty years. Together we have faced everything life has thrown at us, the disappointments and discouragements, the mountain tops and the valleys, the heartaches, the tears, and of course, the joys and the stresses of daily living. We have had some tough days. But we've also had some fun and laughed a good deal together along the way. It's been quite the ride. We did life together, and I wouldn't have it any other way. I am grateful for the years we've had and your steady love for God and me. But mostly, I am thankful to God for Y-O-U, a gift from the Lord of heaven, who in His divine providence saw fit to unite us as one so many years ago. We've grown old together. Let's finish these last few chapters strong and bring a smile to the face of God.

–Sandy

Contents

Introduction: I Am an Old Man 1

Chapter 1: Embrace Your Gray Hair And Be Thankful You Have Any Hair At All 15

Chapter 2: Enjoy The Moment. The Journey Is Short. 25

Chapter 3: Live In The Present. The Good Ole Days Aren't So Good. 33

Chapter 4: Avoid Living On Yesterday's Headlines. You Still Have Something Left To Give Today. 49

Chapter 5: Lean on God. There Is Nothing, Absolutely Nothing, You Can't Trust Him With 55

Chapter 6: Set Your Eyes Toward Heaven. There Is More To Come. 69

Chapter 7: The Grace Of God. I Need Every Bit I Can Get!........ 81

Chapter 8: Feed On The Faithfulness Of God And A Good Slice Of Pizza 95

Chapter 9: Celebrate Life No Matter How Bad It Gets 109

Conclusion: The Time of the End 115

About The Author 123

Other Books By Sanford Zensen 125

"You're going to meet an old man [or woman] someday down the road—ten, thirty, fifty years from now—waiting there for you. You'll be catching up with him [or her]. What kind of old man are you going to meet?

That old man will be you. He'll be the composite of everything you do, say, and think—today and tomorrow. His mind will he see in a mold you have made by your beliefs. His heart will be turning out what you've been putting into it. Every little thought, every deed goes into this old man.

Every day in every way you are becoming more and more like yourself. Open your life to others, think in terms of what you can give, your contribution to life, and the old man grows larger, softer, kindlier, and greater."[2]

—Richard S. Halverson, former U.S. Senate Chaplain

INTRODUCTION

I Am an Old Man

Indeed, what kind of old man or woman will you meet? I'm nearing eighty. I *am* an old man. My heart still feels young, but physically, my body is betraying me. I pee a lot.

My wife and I were at an entertainment venue in Pigeon Forge, Tennessee, watching a variety show and having dinner. It was intermission. I got up and headed for the men's room. No doubt,

---

[2] Daniel Henderson, *The Deeper Life* (Minneapolis, Minnesota: Bethany House, 2014), 165-166.

there was an urgency to my walk. I noticed a young teenager was in front of me as we moved through the crowd. Much to my dismay, he was taking his sweet old time, strolling along without a care in the world, oblivious to my needs. I tapped him on the shoulder and said to him, "Son, let me give you a piece of advice … free. It will cost you nothing. Herre it is. Don't ever get in front of an old man who has to pee. He will run you over!" He smiled and stepped aside. Good move. Depends for Men is not a fashion statement I want to make.

Hard to believe. Life just happened, *"three score and ten,"* seventy years plus…gone! Just like that, in an instant. Moses reminded us

> **Psalm 90:10, NIV** – *Our days may come to seventy years, or eighty, if our strength endures; yet the best of them are but trouble and sorrow, for they quickly pass, and we fly away.*

It seems all too short. Life, indeed, has passed *"quickly,"* which seems like light-speed, and serves only to accentuate the inescapable conclusion that life is about losing. Think about it. With the passing of every year, your testosterone levels drop. Your strength and vitality is on steady decline. Your eyesight grows dim. Your hair falls out. Your teeth are yesterday's news. Your legs give out. Your belly goes to pot (at least, that's what it looks like). The phenomenon is called a "dad bod." I have one of those, and it's not a pretty sight. It's disheartening. Then, you lose your parents. In some cases, your spouse dies after fifty-plus years of marriage. Some sooner. Your friends disappear, and sometimes you bury your child. Your mind is not safe, either. The number of times I find myself searching for the remote, my car keys, or my glasses steadily increases. I forget a lot. About the only thing I've never lost is my weight. I'm working on it, but to no avail. Life never stays the same. It changes. I've changed. You changed. Most of all, you lose today and a zest for living. Yesterday is gone and tomorrow seems to pick up speed with each passing day. Life flies bye.

I remember visiting an elderly woman at the local nursing home. She was confined to her bed. Nellie was ninety-three. No husband. No children. No extended family. And no close friends to speak of … not anymore. She had survived them all. No one was left. As I stood by her bedside, she looked so frail to me.

"Nellie, tell me. You are over ninety. How fast have those years passed?"

She struggled to push herself up from the bed and tried to snap her fingers, which she could no longer do effectively. She so wanted to punctuate her response, but arthritis and weakness had taken their toll on her frail body. Her strength was no more.

She marshaled a response and whispered, "Oh, so very fast. Just like that. The years have flown by. Everything is now gone. My husband is gone. My house is gone, and what few friends I had over the years are all but gone, too."

Nothing was left of yesteryear. Her eyes were sad. A sense of loneliness and heartbreak filled her hospital room while we talked. As a young man and pastor, I didn't fully appreciate then what she said and felt so deeply. I can assure you, that is no longer the case. I get it.

We read in the Scriptures about men like Noah, whose days *"were nine hundred and fifty (years), and he died."* (Genesis 9:29). Such is the case for all flesh and blood. Death marks and mars life in a fallen world.

The fifth chapter of Genesis lists the names of men from each succeeding generation from Adam to Lamech. Their end was the same. The phrase, *"and he died,"* is repeated over and over again to drive the point home. No one escapes. Aging happens, and dying eventually catches us all. Jacob lived 130 years, Moses 120, and both died. Aaron lived 123 years, and Joshua made it to 110. No matter. The end results were the same. And then, there's Methuselah who lived to a ripe old age of 969 years. I cannot even imagine. That's a lot of birthday cake and candles, and yet they all aged and eventually died.

The significance of finishing strong and making the most of the time we have cannot be overstated. Life won't last, at least not here on planet earth. Whatever it is that you and I want to do with whatever time we've got left, with the lives God has given us, we had better get to it and not waste a single day. Perseverance along with purpose and a good dose of reality are necessary right up to the end.

Jocko Willink is a twenty-year veteran of the U.S. Navy Seal teams. On the battlefield, under fire, he learned the importance of staying focused on the mission and hanging in there until the shooting stopped, the fighting ended, and the mission was completed. He said, "Perseverance is key to success in any endeavor, but without perseverance and purpose in combat, there can be no victory."[3] The same goes for our day-to-day lives. *"Anyone who meets a testing challenge head-on and manages to stick it out is mighty fortunate. For such persons… the reward is life and more life"* (James 1:12, MSG). So wrote the half-brother of Jesus.

I'm nowhere near 400-plus years old (thank God), and neither are you, but the need to stay the course and continue to walk with the King right up to the end of our days is significant and vitally important.

After all, this is not ESPN Sports Center. There are no re-runs here. You can't ever go back. So, get it right the first time. The writer of the epistle to the Hebrews put it like this: *"And let us run with endurance the race God has set before us…keeping our eyes on*

---

[3] Dan Schawbel, Jocko Willink: career advice from a former Navy Seal, *Forbes*, Jan 23, 2017, retrieved from
https://www.forbes.com/sites/danschawbel/2017/01/23/jocko-willink-career-advice-from-a-former-navy-seal/

Jesus, the champion who initiates (originates) and perfects our faith (Hebrews 12:1-2, NLT).

One day the life we know will end for us all. Before we know it, the length of our days will come to a screeching halt. There is no avoiding that truth. We are going the way of all flesh. I often get up in the morning, look at myself in the mirror (a rather painful experience), and ask, "Where did that young man go who used to be in there?" The answer is not encouraging, but it is enlightening and honest. "The golden years," it's been said, "are really just metallic years: gold in the tooth, silver in your hair, and lead in the rear."[4] Nice thought.

Recently, I heard David Jeremiah on Moody Radio tell the following story about a birthday card he had received:

> *"It says, 'Hi!' And then you open it and there's a little flap inside. It reads, 'Every year on your birthday, I touch you with my magic wand. And you look one year older.' And I opened it to the center and it said, 'Good night, man. I must have beat the tar out of you.'"*[5]

My kind of story, though it hits a little bit too close to home and bruises my pride.

If the truth be told, I have more years behind me than before, and I don't like it one bit. Some days I'd like to set the clock back a little, though life hasn't always been trouble free. I've had my fair share of tears and heartbreak, setbacks and sorrows. It has not always been easy, but I love life. I embrace it, want it, and am eager for it. I've never wanted to become a grumpy old, bitter, angry man, struggling with depression over what could have been or what once

---

[4] Chrissy Peterson, Recreation Director, Recreation Department, Senior citizens jokes, *Town of Hudson, NH*, retrieved from https://www.hudsonnh.gov/recreation/page/senior-citizens-jokes.

[5] David Jeremiah, Happy are the hurting, *Turning Point, Moody Radio Chattanooga*, February 7, 2024, retrieved from https://www.davidjeremiah.org/radio.

was. It's an ugly sight. I've met one, too many men over the years who could not shouldered the weight of grievances, resentments, and disappointments, and in the process, developed an ugly disposition—unhappy, frustrated, and defiant. It's too much for anyone to bear and much too costly. I'd rather grow old with some sense of dignity, grace, and a genuine appreciation for the days God has afforded me, for the family I have enjoyed, and the people I've gotten to know and shared life and ministry with through the years. I want to finish the "race" strong. Like Enoch, let it be said of me, *"He walked with God"* (Genesis 5:24).

One senior citizen remarked to me,

> *I have a general philosophy of not being complacent about becoming "old"- not letting myself go physically; being up for fun, even if it ventures a bit into the "wild and crazy" side here and there; doing things with my grandchildren that delight them (and me) ...most grandmas don't intentionally stay young at heart. There, you got me on one of my soapboxes!*[6]

Preach on, girl. "Wild and crazy." I'm up for that. I want to die empty…empty of all reserve, all resources, all resolve. Nothing left in the tank. Nothing more to give. Everything depleted, used up, completely spent. It's the only way to live … and the only way to die with few regrets and no self-pity.

I'm not interested in bellyaching about the past nor unduly worrying over my future. This much I know. Eternity and the glory and riches of heaven await. I long to meet the Savior face to face, but not just yet. I want to live fully, passionately, purposefully while the opportunity presents itself. And when it's over and I stand before the divine Tribunal to give an account of how I lived the life He gave me, I want to hear loud and clear from the mouth of God, *"Well*

---

[6] Sharon Vander Drift, Sharon's Facebook Post, Facebook, December 18, 2016.

done, good and faithful servant" (Matthew 25:21, NIV). There are no better words for any man or woman to hear.

When David was nearing death, he informed his son Solomon that he was dying. He said, *"I am going where everyone on earth must someday go* (to the grave). *Take courage and be a man"* (1 Kings 1-2, NLT). I love those last three words, *"Be a man."* They are important. They carry the key to life's success. Permit me to summarize David's words. "Man up, son. Suck it up, buttercup. Stop the whining and complaining. Get your thumb out of your mouth, and make the most of the life you have. It will pass quickly." Great advice for running the "race" to win and finishing life strong. But David didn't stop there. There was more. He told Solomon how to do it and live successfully. Here is what he said and what we need to know.

> **1 Kings 2:1-3, NLT** – *"Observe the requirements of the Lord your God, and follow all his ways (throughout all your days). Keep the decrees, commands, regulations, and laws written in the Law of Moses so that you will be successful in all you do and wherever you go."*

That about sums up the means to successful Christian living all the days of your life right up to the day you leave this world and enter the gates of eternity. Regardless of what generation you and I live in (old or new), live life God's way and you will always get God's results, a lesson old codgers who have walked with God for some time have known.

As I recall, I was a lot smarter when I was younger. Stop laughing. So were you. It wasn't long, however, before I found out I wasn't all that bright. I was infected with a disease common to youth—inexperience. The symptoms were evident; a self-inflated ego and self-approved folly—in short, nonsense and foolishness. Abraham Lincoln said, "It is better to be silent and be thought a fool, than to speak and remove all doubt." I spoke too soon, one too many times. Lincoln may have borrowed that idea from Solomon who wrote: *"Even fools are thought wise when they keep silent; with their mouths shut, they seem intelligent"* (Proverbs 17:28, NLT). That stings.

No doubt, my mouth has gotten me into more trouble than I care to admit. Let it be known; I have often eaten my words. Not a particularly tasty morsel.

In reality, I was untested in life, unaware of the ruts and pitfalls of daily living, inexperienced in the ways of the world, unfamiliar with real success and the hard lessons of failure. And to make matters worse, I was full of myself. I thought I knew everything there was to know about life, and nobody could tell me otherwise. I lacked humility and good old fashion wisdom. Mark Twain admitted, "When I was a boy of 14, my father was so ignorant I could hardly stand to have the old man around. But when I got to be 21, I was astonished at how much the old man had learned in seven years.[7]

I heard Howard Hendricks of Dallas Theological Seminary define the biblical concept of wisdom as "the art of skillful living,"[8] which I might add is needed at any age— a workable, practical approach to daily life and choosing the right path that leads to success and ultimate victory in our personal and professional lives. The *"abundant life"* (see John 10:10) is what Jesus called it… a life that works well yesterday, today, and tomorrow. Truth never changes.

Life experience is a great teacher, at times a tough but effective master. Here are some humorous and outrageous things I've learned

---

[7] Short freestanding item, Bringing up father, Reader's Digest, (Pleasantville, New York: *The Reader's Digest Association*, September 1937) 22, retrieved from https://quoteinvestigator.com/2010/10/10/twain-father/.

[8] Robert L. Thomas, New American Standard Hebrew-Aramaic and Greek Dictionaries, # 2451, retrieved from Logos Bible Software 4, Platinum, 2001-2010.

Introduction: I Am an Old Man

(sometimes the hard way) from my nearly eighty years of life on planet earth.

- "At my age, flowers scare me." George Burns, comedian.
- Some days you're the dog; other days you're the fire hydrant.
- "The older I get, the more clearly I remember things that never happened." Mark Twain.
- The only time the world beats a path to my door is when I'm in the bathroom.
- "First you forget names, then you forget faces, then you forget to pull your zipper up, then you forget to pull your zipper down." Leo Rosenberg
- "When your friends begin to flatter you on how young you look, it's a sure sign you're getting old." - Mark Twain
- As I've grown older, I've become "like an old car—more and more repairs and replacements are necessary." - C.S. Lewis
- If I could tell my younger self one thing about living in this world, it would be – learn to duck! Keifer Sutherland
- "The older I get, the better I used to be." Lee Trevino, PGA Legend. [9]
- You should always go to other people's funerals, otherwise, they won't come to yours. Yogi Berra

I love those. They make me smile. Humor is good for the soul.

Here is a partial list of the more serious lessons learned from personal observation, from the things I've read, and a few things I've heard— everyday wisdom from experienced people with little

---

[9] Some statements listed by Porter Simon, an attorney (and other similar sites), Very funny quotes about aging, Porter Simon Law, May 19, 2023, retrieved from https://portersimon.com/very-funny-quotes-about-aging/.

"tread-life left on their tires." They are presented in no particular order. They are little nuggets of truth and advice for the younger set, but also solid lessons for those who have lived out much of their lives and are now wondering how they are going to recapture life, regain some sense of vitality, and rework their dreams, especially when they may feel like life has passed them by.

- Get up! Failure is not fatal. Another day ... another chance ... to get it right.
- Never take tomorrow for granted. You may never get there.
- My mother was right...Life is unfair. Get over it.
- Life is worth living no matter how hard it gets.
- Spend your life investing in people, because that's what Jesus did. There is no better way to live.
- Trust God. He always delivers His best for my best. Count on it.
- "Jesus loves me, this I know, for the Bible tells me so." An old Sunday School chorus with a message of truth we all need to hear.
- Forgive, but never forget. God does it just like that. So should you.
- Make peace with your past so it won't screw up the present.
- The most important thing in life is your relationship to God. Everything, and I mean everything, flows from that.
- Build treasure in heaven. The interest rates are out of this world. (Matthew 6:19-20).
- Honor Christ with your life, and God the Father will honor you (John 12:26).

Here's a few more compiled by my friend and colleague, Dr. Bill Brown, former president of Bryan College and Cedarville University, and a Senior Fellow of Worldview and Culture, and Dean of the Colson Fellows Program. They are insightful and highly pertinent to my daily life and yours no matter what my age.

- I have learned that there are no shortcuts to any place worth going.
- I have learned to believe in miracles.
- I have learned that when someone believes in you, you can do almost anything.
- I have learned that when you ask God to use you today He will.
- I have learned that it's not what you have in your life but who you have in your life that counts.
- I've learned that it's not what happens to people that's important. It's what they do about it.[10]
- I have learned that God usually redeems us through our sufferings, not from them.

Great stuff when moving through the days and years ahead, and life is unfolding at a quickening, unrelenting pace.

When I was a young man working as a lifeguard in upstate New York (yes, I had the bronzed body for that back then), I met an elderly gentleman while patrolling the lake front. The man had been retired for a number of years. I asked him what he did for a living. He told me. I asked, "How long did you do that?" He said, "For thirty-five years. I responded, "You mean to tell me that you worked at the same place doing the same thing, for the same company, for thirty-five years? You must have loved it." How naïve I was. His response was brutally honest. He looked me straight in the eye and

---

[10] William Brown, "Things I Have Learned," Used by permission.

said bluntly, "I hated every blankety-blank minute of it." A sad tale of hapless days and apparently there were lots of them. His latter years were not much better. I walked away thanking God for showing me what I didn't want for my life. I didn't want to simply make a living. I wanted to make a life. I still do in my closing years.

Hall of Famer and former Yankee catcher, Yogi Berra once said, "It ain't over 'til it's over." It certainly isn't. Not for me, and not for you, as long as there is breath in our bodies.

Donald Trump took the oath for President of the USA on January 20, 2025. It was his second time, making him the oldest man to ever be sworn in to the highest office of the land to lead the most powerful and influential country in the world. A remarkable accomplishment for a man his age. His enemies had written him off. They tried to bury him in the court system (still trying), and then attempted to shoot him dead. But at the age of seventy-eight he staged what many consider to be the greatest political comeback of all time. Neither politics, the woke agenda, nor age stopped him. He pressed forward into the White House with unrelenting determination and vigor. Berra was right; "It ain't over 'til it's over." You go, old people!

As long as there is life in these old bones, I'm going to grab hold of every event, every occasion before me. I want to run the race. I want to wring every ounce of laughter and tears from the day. I want to live under God's authority and sovereignty—looking forward to the rising of the sun each day with joy in the morning, because God in His providence has given me and you another day, another chance, another opportunity.

After a disappointing loss (November 23, 2024) to football powerhouse, the Kansas Jayhawks, Head Coach of the University of Colorado Buffalos Dion Sanders, said this in an ESPN interview following the game:

When you are in control of your own destiny, it's a phenomenal thing. I don't think about football. I think about life. The lesson for these boys (team) is this. If God grants you everything you need in life, all the abilities, the thought processes, the visuals (and the resources, and if you are capable of seeing and doing what needs to be done), and you don't do anything with it, that's on you.[11]

Absolutely. We are all responsible for what we are able and equipped to do regardless of age. No more, and certainly, no less.

Here are a few recommendations for growing old with grace and finishing strong. Let them challenge you to make the most of the years, months, days or even hours you have left. See what God can do with a man or woman who is determined to live life as He intended—with meaning, purpose, faith, and hope for today, and for tomorrow, and for all the tomorrows to come. Listen up, people … you can do this.

1. Embrace Your Grey Hair And Be Thankful You Have Any Hair At All.
2. Enjoy The Moment. The Journey Is Short.
3. Live In The Present. The Good Ole Days Aren't So Good.
4. Avoid Living On Yesterday's Headlines. You Have More To Give.
5. Lean On God. There Is Nothing, Absolutely Nothing, You And God Can't Handle.
6. Set Your Eyes Toward Heaven. There Is More To Come.
7. The Grace Of God. I Need Every Bit I Can Get!
8. Feed On The Faithfulness Of God And A Good Slice Of Pizza.

---

[11] ESPN TV interview, November 23, 2024.

9. Celebrate Life No Matter How Bad It Gets.

"For everything there is a season," so observed Solomon, a very wise man. He wrote:

> **Ecclesiastes 3:1-11 NLT** – *" For everything there is a season, a time for every activity under heaven, a time to be born and a time to die. A time to plant and a time to harvest... A time to cry and a time to laugh. A time to grieve and a time to dance...Yet God has made everything beautiful for its own time"*

Growing old is no exception to the rule. Your life and mine is a *beautiful* thing. God made it. Let's meet our latter years with a little grace, a little dignity, and a whole lot of gratitude for the years we've been permitted to experience—for length of days, for joy of heart, for the privilege of serving the King and His kingdom, and for the marvelous love of God that has taken us thus far.

Pick up your cane. Grab the handles of your walker, if necessary, and off you go. Finish strong, and make the most of the years you've got left.

"Teach us to number our days, that we may gain a heart of wisdom."

–Psalm 90:12, NIV (David)

CHAPTER 1

Embrace Your Gray Hair And Be Thankful You Have Any Hair At All

Put down the Rogaine, the L'Oreal, and the Just for Men. Your gray hair should serve as evidence of life and wisdom (hopefully) which only comes with longevity, that is, walking with God over the long haul. There is no shortcut or substitute for experience, for faith learned and exercised throughout the years, for the acquired knowledge of the presence and character of Almighty God, and the repeated observations of His personal intervention infused into the details of your daily life. David wrote,

> **Isaiah 46:4 NIV** – *"Even to your old age and gray hairs (and I've got a head of those) I am He (God), I am He who will sustain you (bear your burdens). I have made you and I will carry (or lift) you; I will sustain you and I will rescue (deliver) you."*

A great promise straight from the mouth of God Himself. Clearly, a life lived for and with God is not a series of unrelated, haphazard events, nor is it an accumulation of cosmic accidents occurring without divine rhyme or reason. There may be mysteries popping up along the way in our personal lives, unexplained, even tragic circumstances or trials, but none of it has caught God unaware or surprised. To the contrary, your life represents God's perfect design and constant attendance to the affairs of daily living. The sovereignty of God is no joke. You have been made to live under His rulership and influence, made for this world and the next, including old age, the twilight years, as you near the close of your earthly life. God has every hair numbered on your head (No doubt, some of us have more than others). He has seen fit in His presence and power to *"sustain"* you and me through the years. Your grey hair is evidence of that fact—God's provision, His wisdom, and power energizing your daily affairs. Embrace it and cherish every moment God has given you.

Zacharias and his wife Elizabeth were *"advanced in years"* (Luke 1:7), childless, and well beyond childbearing age. Yesteryear had slipped by with little notice. One day, while Zacharias was performing his priestly duties (burning incense) in the temple, an angel of the Lord stopped in and tapped him on the shoulder. He had a message from God that would change the life of the priest in his later years—a sure word from heaven that would give him and his wife a new perspective, a new direction, a new plan, along with some diapers, bottles, baby formula, a stroller, a bassinet, a child seat for the chariot, and of course the much needed pacifier to dip in honey to shut the baby up. Excessive crying is annoying and sleepless nights are no fun.

Nobody saw it coming. Zacharias' wife would bear a son in their old age whose name would be John. *"And you,"* God's messenger would say, *"will have joy and gladness, and many will rejoice at his birth. For he will be great in the sight of the Lord...and he will turn back many of the sons of Israel to the Lord their God"* (Luke 1:13-16). What Jewish mother wouldn't want to hear that about their son?

It must have sounded good to an old man, too, if not a bit crazy and exciting. Who would have thought?

Zacharias needed reassurance. He needed to know that God would use him (gray hair and all) in the days ahead to do the impossible, something so extraordinary, so unusual, so unexpected that there would be no doubt that this was God's assignment and God's will for an old man and his wife. Know *"for certain"* seniors (Luke 1:18) that God is up to something good, something uncommon in your personal life. And like Zacharias, a new adventure is ahead. Drop the skepticism. Meet the challenges. Trust God with your closing years. Make no mistake. His desire has always been for your well-being. A reminder Zacharias needed. Where would he and his wife fit into God's schemes? Where and how could the man continue to be of service to God and His kingdom? He would soon find out. The divine message is unmistakable and applicable for every servant of God who desires to serve the interests' of heaven.

As with the old man Zacharias, God is not through with you just yet. You have not breathed your last. Life has not ended. There is still more, much more, for you to do that is of great value and service to people and God's kingdom. Go find your niche. Roll up your sleeves. Get cracking.

"No one ever does anything he doesn't want to do" so wrote Hugh Downs, former host of ABC's *20/20*. That makes each of us responsible for our choices and actions in life and the integration of beliefs into daily practice. [12] The epistle of James puts it like this: *"But prove yourselves doers of the word and not merely hearers who delude themselves"* (James 1:22). Word and deed. I am accountable for both. I am without excuse regardless of age.

---

[12] Phillip L. Berman, Editor *The Courage of Conviction,* (New York, New York: Ballantine, 1985, 1986). 80-81.

Dr. Wayne Dyer, New York Times bestselling author and motivational speaker, revealed the one common denominator he discovered among men and women considered to be great people and high achievers. He noted, "None of them died with their music still in them."[13] And neither should we. I want to be able to say at the conclusion of my life that I've used every bit of what God has graciously and abundantly given me. I've wasted nothing. I've used it all to further His interests. I've done what I could, what I must—to leave my little corner of the world a bit better for having lived in it. Lord, so order my life, right up to the end, that I might complete the tasks assigned to me by You.

From his deathbed, Ivan Illyich, assessed his very existence, his personal journey, decisions, experiences, and his own mortality. Tolstoy wrote in his classic story, *The Death of Ivan Ilyich,*

> *... the whole arrangement of his life and of his family, and all his social and official interests, might all have been false. He tried to defend all those things to himself and suddenly felt the weakness of what he was defending. There was nothing to defend. He had not spent his life living as he should have done.*

A telling, painful conclusion. Ilyich posed this pointed question to his wife: "What if I have really been wrong in the way I have lived my whole life?"[14] A terrible, troubling thought— to think that the man may have missed life's best, to have lived and failed one's conscience, to have lost sight of dreams and hopes, his marriage and family, and of course, God.

It is inconceivable to me to have lived the better part of my life only to have come up short, and to have squandered my opportunity

---

[13] Sean Craxton, The quote of the day show, Daily Motivational Talks, retrieved from https://open.spotify.com/show/1tA9C1DNuxu9ULG8yVS70x

[14] Leo Tolstoy, The Death of Ilyich and Other Stories, Translated by Ronald Wilks, Anthony Briggs, and David McDuff, London, England: Penguin Classics, 2008), 213.

to get the most from the years afforded to me. To think that I may have failed God, the Giver of life and all that is good, the One to whom I must give an account for the choices I've made and my unwillingness to complete my God-given mission in life is intolerable. How very tragic and unthinkable to have "lived my whole life" out of step with the God, *"who loved me and delivered Himself up for me"* (Galatians 2:20).

Ilyich had left too much undone. His focus was unclear. His values and goals were warped. His efforts, misplaced. I can relate to it all. But here is the Good News; I may have blown it along the way, but by the grace and mercy of God who redeems my past, I can make the present and my closing years (or days) better than its start.

The Apostle Paul knew God intimately. He knew of His love, mercy, and grace, and He knew of God's promise never to leave him nor forsake him. Others would, but not God. While locked in a Roman prison, Paul wrote. *"The Lord is near"* (Philippians 4:4-5). How comforting. That fact alone is cause for great *"rejoicing."* God is involved in my life every day, in every way, and everywhere. Whether I'm young starting kindergarten at five years old, or old strapped to a nursing home bed so I won't fall out ... God has always been here and there, near and far, always, at all times, to set me upon a sure path that follows His leading and brings me to this very day and beyond. Through the ups and downs of daily living, we all must endure the hardships, the trials, the tough times and the good times, the climb to the pinnacle of success and the falling down into the valley of defeat, the tears and the joys. Through it all God has had His hand upon you to guide you every step of the way, lift you above the pain and disappointments to preserve your life through the years, to this very day, and get you to where He wants you to be. Your life has been divinely calculated, designed, charted, and planned out in detail. You have not been engaged in haphazard living, chance encounters, or unexpected events. Your life is no accident or no surprise to God. If you walk with God, you are not drifting aimlessly from day to day, carried about with no real reason or destination in mind. Quite the opposite. Look closer. There is a sense of divine stability in every grey hair I see. There is security, focus, and a purpose for the days I have lived and the days before me. And for that, I am thankful, hopeful, and encouraged.

In his prime, Mike Tyson may have been the best heavyweight boxer who ever put on a pair of gloves to climb into the ring, a devastating puncher, who knocked out forty of his opponents, many in the first round. He referred to himself has a natural-born killer. He is now fifty-eight years old with a greying beard. He recently stepped back into the ring to fight a man half his age. He lost on a decision. No surprise there. It was expected. Nobody really thought otherwise. After all, the years do take their toll physically on us all. Admittedly, I was hoping for a miracle (along with millions of others), pulling for the old man. He was one of us seniors. The miracle didn't happen. Regardless, Tyson had reached the heights of the boxing profession years ago. Championship titles, fame, and fortune followed him everywhere. By most modern standards, he was a professional success, though his personal life significantly suffered. He is a legend, an icon. In an interview, Mike Tyson was talking about death to a fourteen-year-old reporter who asked him about what sort of a legacy he would like to leave behind once his career was finally over. His response was revealing.

> *(A legacy) means absolutely nothing to me. I'm just passing through. I'm going to die and it's going to be over. Who cares about legacy after that?...We're just dead. We're dust. We're absolutely nothing. Our legacy is nothing* [15]

---

[15] Daniel Trainor, Mike Tyson's interview with teen reporter about legacy goes viral: "We're just dead," US Weekly, November 15, 2024, retrieved from https://www.usmagazine.com/entertainment/news/mike-tysons-interview-with-teen-reporter-about-legacy-goes-viral/

A sad place to be, especially for a man who had surveyed the last sixty years of his life and saw nothing behind or before him of any consequence and real value. You live. You die. That's it. Nothing in life really matters, including a world heavyweight title. Franklin Graham said of the interview:

> *I hope I can meet Mike Tyson someday—I want him to know the truth. Each one of us has a soul that is going to live for eternity in one of two places—Heaven or Hell. The only way you can be sure that your soul is secure in the hands of God is by putting your faith and trust in His Son, Jesus Christ. God sent His Son from heaven to this earth to pay the penalty for our sins. Jesus shed His blood on the cross for your sins and mine. He died, was buried, and on the third day God raised Him back to life. If you will simply believe this by faith and ask God to forgive you, He will, and you can spend eternity in His presence in Heaven. My prayer is that Mike Tyson—or anyone reading this—will make the decision right now to put your faith and trust in the Lord Jesus Christ. That's a win that lasts for eternity.*[16]

The Caleb of the Bible is my hero. At eighty-five years old he did not shrink back from his future, nor did he pine away, feeling sorry for himself for the forty years of wondering in the desert he had to endure. Instead, he looked at his past and clearly saw the hand of God at work in his life. Do likewise.

Earlier, he had been sent by Moses to spy out the promised land and report back his findings and recommendations, which he did. His conclusions were definitive. His motives were pure—move people from unbelief to belief, from darkness to light, from fear to faith, from death to life. Through the eyes of faith in the words and character of God, Caleb immediately recognized what could be. He had seen what God had promised…Canaan *"flowing with milk and*

---

[16] Franklin Graham, Facebook, Nov 15, 2024.

honey" (Numbers 14:8, NKJV), a good, rich, fertile land. He also saw fortified cities and the inhabitants of the land—a fierce people, giants, strong, and formidable who would strike fear in the hearts of their enemies. But not Caleb. None of it was of any consequence to an old man who knew God intimately. He set his mind on the God of Creation, who made heaven and earth with but His word, who commands the armies of heaven, who is fearful and more powerful than kings and pharaohs, rich men and beggars, prophets and priests, philosophers and the lowly believer. None could possibly ever imagine or conceive of a God that big, that mighty, that awesome. He *is* God, the One without equal, who laughs at the armies of men trying to challenge His rulership, strip Him of His authority, and ultimately to remove Him from the throne of the universe and beyond (see Psalm 2:1-5). Not happening ... ever.

It was this God that Caleb heard speak years ago on a journey through the desert. He had watched with wonder and awe the supernatural, mighty power of God unleashed upon Egypt that had brought it to its knees. Nothing can stand against the lordship of God and His word and will. At the water's edge of the Red Sea, God leveled the mightiest army in the ancient world. For decades, Caleb had witnessed God's continual provision for His people, quenching their thirst in the desert, giving them manna and meat to eat when their stomachs were empty, and kept their shoes from wearing out. There were no doubts about who God was, is, and forever will be. *"The Lord is with us,"* Caleb confidently declared, *"Do not fear them"* (Numbers 14:9). That was his report at forty years of age. Take note. Forty-five years later, nothing has changed. God is still God.

God's character and person remained the same. Caleb's faith grew exponentially with each passing year. His faith was confirmed with every step he took. His resolve was fixed. His courage was strengthened and anchored to the promises and power of God. The lessons he learned as the years passed would serve him well in his old age, as it must be with the rest of us. Caleb was not created for a rocking chair. He was prepared to press forward to be used of God in his old age to make a difference in his world and the generations to come.

By now, Caleb had put some years behind him. He said of himself, *"I am still as strong today as I was in the day of Moses…as my strength was then, so my strength is now, for war … give me this mountain"* (Joshua 14:10-11). And so, I pray:

> *Lord, I want that same spirit at the close of my life. I want to stay in the battle for as long as I can, and fight the good fight (2 Timothy 4:7). I want new mountains to climb and new challenges to meet. I want to be found at Your coming dressed in my work clothes, not my pajamas, or be clothed in "the armor of God," as a warrior in Your kingdom, armed with "mighty weapons…to knock down the strongholds of human reasoning and to destroy false arguments…(and) rebellious thoughts" raised up by hell's clever schemes to "keep people from knowing (You)" (2 Corinthians 10:3-5, NLT). I want to unsheathe "the sword of the Spirit, which is the word of God," and hold up the "shield of faith" (see Ephesians 6:11-15) in order to deflect the devil's arrows designed to discourage, disappoint, and to defeat my advancement in the holy cause of Your mission.*
>
> *Laid up in bed with whatever divine strength I've got left, let me stay in the fight for as long as I can, and "pray at all times in the Spirit" (Ephesians 6:18). Pray hard. Pray fervently. Pray frequently even from the confines of a wheelchair or laying on my back in a hospital bed sick as a dog. If praying is all I can do, that will be enough.*
>
> *At the end of my days, I may not have much breath or strength left in my body. But let there always remain within me a deep desire, a holy drive to do what I can, what I must, to be useful to You in disrupting the reign of*

wickedness in this world. In the process, let me gain a good reputation in hell (Ephesians 6:12). That's what I want—to embrace my grey hair and be thankful to You, Lord, that I have any left on my head, grateful to heaven that I may still be productive and helpful in some manner to a cause much greater than myself.

"If you can't fly," said Martin Luther King, Jr., "then run. If you can't run, then walk. If you can't walk, then crawl, but whatever you do, you have to keep moving." I have to be *"in My Father's house"* (lit. *in the things of My Father* - Luke 2:49, NASB), attending to God's business and His affairs.

Don't stop. Embrace the life given to you by God. Get into His *business.* Leave a good legacy behind. Make a difference in the world before you run out of time. Don't sweat the grey hair. Be glad you still got some.

We shall have all eternity to celebrate the victories, but we have only the few hours before sunset in which to win them."

–Amy Carmichael

CHAPTER 2

Enjoy The Moment. The Journey Is Short.

Life happens at blinding speed— here today; gone tomorrow. You may not like it, but that's how it works. You know it, and so do I. Woody Allen was asked about his own aging and sense of mortality:

> *It (getting old) is a bad business. It's a confirmation that the anxieties and terrors I've had all my life were accurate. There's no advantage to aging. You don't get wiser, you don't get more mellow, you don't see life in a more glowing way. You have to fight your body decaying, and you have less options.*[17]

A sad commentary by a man obviously without joy, absent of hope, and void of purpose. You live to die, and then … nothing. Pack it in. The ride is over. Maybe there are a few thrills along the way, like a rollercoaster at the amusement park, but it all quickly comes to a screeching halt in just a few moments. Nobody would be happy

---

[17] The Week Staff, Allen on aging, *The Week,* January 8, 2015, retrieved from https://theweek.com/articles/471539/allen-aging.

with that worldview, including Woody Allen with all of his success, fame, and money. The brevity and fragility of life vividly comes into play for us all.

My wife and I met some friends for lunch a few weeks ago. We had such a good time together, enjoying each other's company, laughing, and talking about our grandkids. It was wonderful. We planned to do it again sometime soon. Unfortunately, it never happened. The woman was hospitalized a few weeks after our lunch meeting. She was diagnosed with stomach cancer. Suddenly, the laughing stopped. Her dreams vanished. Her hopes were vanquished. She never recovered. Without warning, the disease manifested itself for a second time in her life. One moment she was talking with her husband and friends and looking forward to the future and the next she was fighting for her life. The opportunity to be together again this side of eternity was lost. I felt cheated. I know her husband certainly did.

Job said, *"My life is but a breath"* (Job 7:7), which might be the understatement of centuries past. How right he was. David wrote, *"For my days pass away like smoke, and my bones burn like a furnace"* (Psalm 102:3, ESV. James reminded us that our life is but *"a vapor that appears for a little while and then vanishes away"* (James 4:14). The end comes swiftly, and the journey is short. There is no promise that we are guaranteed tomorrow. Even more reason to enjoy life and make our days count now, making the journey as important as the destination. Frankly, there is no time to waste.

If we are to make a difference in our corner of the world—contributing, impacting, influencing, assisting, and helping wherever and whenever God gives us opportunity in our later years, we must look to Him for direction and strength. The days fly by at break-neck speed.

Nelson Mandela was seventy-five years old when he was awarded the Nobel Peace prize in 1993 and elected president of South Africa, and this after thirty years in prison for opposing apartheid, a political policy and practice of blatant racism within the government.[18] Golda Meir was seventy-one when she became prime minister of Israel. Joshua was eighty-seven years old when he led Israel into the promised land of Canaan. Martin Luther was thirty-four when he lit the fires of the Reformation. He died at sixty-two. What fortitude and perseverance, all of them—men and women who accomplished much in their lifetimes. I am without excuse, whether I'm thirty or eighty plus years old. There is no time to waste. I can still smile and laugh. I can still speak a word of encouragement. I can still walk with a friend through the valley of despair and loneliness. I can climb mountains, maybe not as fast as I used to, but I can still find a place in God's kingdom and help people succeed. I've got more to give.

Abram had already logged seventy years of living when God knocked on his front door to deliver a message: *"Go forth…I will make you a great nation"* (Genesis 11:4). Now Abram was comfortable, well established, and wealthy, *"very rich in livestock, in silver and in gold"* (Genesis 13:1). It would have made no difference had he been penniless. As an old man by today's standards, Abram was a man with a God-given destiny laid in his lap. God promised him, *"Your reward shall be great"* (Genesis 15:1). A good word for any man at any age and any level of prosperity or potential. Whether you are a shut-in, confined to your bed and unable to leave your house or hospital room or a person with all your physical and/or mental faculties, you are privileged to serve the interests of God and people in some specific capacity and place. Wherever you find yourself, at whatever age or condition, you have a place and a job serving God. Don't sell yourself short.

---

[18] Marika Price Spitulski, Never too old to succeed: inspiring people who achieved great things later in life, *Nice News,* May 20, 2023, retrieved from https://nicenews.com/culture/people-achieved-great-things-later-life/.

My mother-in-law Irene had a wonderful ministry to nursing home patients, and she was in her nineties at the time, still driving, still visiting, still caring, still praying, still encouraging, still sharing the hope and love of Jesus. She was a remarkable woman doing faithfully and wholeheartedly what she had done all her life— serving the church and the community. She "seized the moment" as God presented to her the opportunities, resources, and abilities to be productive. Not much had changed since her early, child evangelism days: just the place and form of kingdom work. She closed out her life as she had lived it: finding her niche in serving God and people. Do the same. Find your place, and you *"will dwell in the house of the Lord forever"* (Psalm 23:6).

Following the great Chicago fire on October 8, 1871, D.L. Moody went to London in 1872 for rest and study. He had no intention of preaching during his stay, but he did. The service at a local church in London did not go well. The people were apathetic, bored, and unresponsive. No spiritual punch was evident. Moody was sorry he ever agreed to fill the pulpit. There was, however, a woman in the city who had been asking God to send Moody from America to London. She was a house-bound invalid and eventually was hospitalized. Her name was Marianne Adlard. Her sister told her that Mr. Moody had come from Chicago and preached that morning in her church. The woman said it was an answer to her prayers, and despite her sickness she fasted and prayed for his ministry the rest of the day, asking God to use him that evening. As a little, frail, sickly woman prayed, the power and presence of God fell greatly that night with supernatural results as Moody preached. Four or five hundred people responded to the gospel message. Ms. Adlard vowed to continue praying for him (Moody) until the day one of them died. Moody was never the same. He preached to millions with extraordinary clarity and power.[19] Adlard overcame her limitations to serve the interests of God's kingdom. She "seized the moment." So can you and I, as God gives us eyes to see and the ability to serve Him in any capacity He deems necessary. Prayer and a willing heart gets amazing results.

New York Times bestselling author and president of Proverbs 31 Ministries, Lysa TerKeurst, wrote about the power and necessity of prayer in bringing about significant change in our lives:

Prayer opens my spiritual eyes to see things I can't see on my own. (And so it was for Abraham). And I'm convinced prayer matters. Prayers are powerful and effective...prayer does make a difference — a life-changing, mind-blowing, earth-rattling difference. We don't need to know how. We don't need to know when. We just need to kneel confidently and know the tremors of simple prayers extend far-wide and far-high and far-deep.[20]

Marianne Adlard would understand.

One day God and Abraham got to talking about life and what God desired for his future. God spoke. Abraham listened. That's as it should be. Consequently, God turned the man's life upside down. That must have been some kind of prayer meeting.

As a result, Abraham packed up, took what he needed, left for Canaan, and didn't look back. He did what he was told, a pretty good move for any man at any age, complying with divine orders. No questions asked. No excuses. No complaints were ever recorded or lodged with heaven. No uncertainty about his decision. He boldly went where few men would go, and stepped out in faith. He trusted

---

[19] Jordan Standridge, The prayers of one faithful lady availeth much, *The Cripple Gate*, May 17, 2016, retrieved from https://thecripplegate.com/.

[20] Lysa TerKeurst, I'm scared to pray boldly, Proverbs 31 Ministries, May 25, 2017, retrieved from https://lysaterkeurst.com/2017/05/25/im-scared-to-pray-boldly/#:~:text=So%2C%20prayer%20does%20make%20a,%2Dhigh%20and%20far%2Ddeep.

God. *"When everything was hopeless, Abraham believed anyway, deciding to live not on the basis of what he saw he couldn't do but on what God said he would do"* (Romans 4:18, MSG). Abraham could have captained the starship *Enterprise* of the Star Trek TV series, whose five-year mission was "to explore strange new worlds; to seek out new life and new civilizations; to boldly go where no man has gone before!"[21] Abraham did just that and set out on an adventure not knowing where he was going and where it would end. He left knowing only that God would be orchestrating his life from his first step to his last and that is precisely how God operates. He is doing the same in your life and mine, regardless of our age or surrounding circumstances. Abraham's courage and trust in God was nothing short of remarkable. *"He did not waver in unbelief."* God called it *"righteousness"*—right thinking and a right attitude that leads to right actions (Romans 4:16-21). There was no hint of a soft retirement in God's instructions, even for a man pushing eighty. No rest homes. No assisted living, or life-care centers on the horizon. Not for Abraham. Nothing. Zero. Just the drive and opportunity to remain available and open to the call of God to be useful, productive, and excited about what the future might hold in the days and months ahead. As an old man, I need that.

That's what I want. Slow down? No, thank you! Not a chance. I want more in the morning when I open my eyes than a cup of coffee and the local news and weather. There must be more. The sanctity and brevity of life hits too close to home and demands an all-out effort while the opportunity exists. More than 150 years ago, ordained minister, philosopher, and politician, who revitalized the city of Birmingham (UK), George Dawson (1821-1876), prayed

---

[21] Gary Martin, To boldly go where no man has gone before, *Phrase Finder*, No date given, retrieved from
https://www.phrases.org.uk/meanings/385400.html.

Our days are Thine, let them be spent for Thee. Our days are few, let them be spent with care ... Lord, we go to our daily work; help us to take pleasure therein. Show us clearly what our duty is; help us to be faithful doing it. Let all we do be well done, fit for Thine eye to see.[22]

Solid, everyday priorities.

How we live our lives, the decisions we make, the roads we take, the places we go, the pursuit of our heart matters greatly. Life marches on ... no matter what. Solomon once observed, *"There is a season for everything."* I'm sure his observation included a cup of hot coffee and a slice of apple crumb cheesecake. There is always time for that.

Seriously, the close of my life and yours will come quicker than any of us would like to think. The *"dust"* (that's you and me) will return to the earth as it was, and the spirit will return to God who gave it (Ecclesiastes 12:7). So, keep moving forward. Don't wind down while there is still breath in your body. Find something productive to do with the time you've got left. Keep pace. Finish strong. Stay active as much as your body and mind will allow. Do what you can, when you can. Complete your mission. No need to do more. No excuses to do less.

Near the close of the play *Macbeth* (Act V, Scene 5), written by William Shakespeare, Macbeth received word that His wife, Lady Macbeth, had committed suicide. He knew his own death was fast approaching, as his enemies closed in for their final assault. He reflected back and assessed his own life. His conclusions were tragic, coming from a man who saw no real purpose and no meaning to his life. His days were for naught. In the end, he would die. His life but a "brief candle." His assessment was on point.

---

[22] Joy L. O'Toole, A wrench in the works, *Myriads of Thought,* January 5, 2015, retrieved from https://joylotoole.org/2015/01/05/a-wrench-in-the-works/.

> *Life's but a walking shadow, a poor player, that struts and frets his hour upon the stage, and then is heard no more; it is a tale told by an idiot, full of sound and fury, signifying nothing.*

Sad. Having spent your life with no sense of value and worth attached to a single day. That's nihilism in its rawest form. I don't buy it.

Though the body may revolt and scream, "Enough!" in its old age, the spirit of a man or woman remains alive, learning to live in full and complete dependence upon God and His faithfulness toward you and me. And that ain't so bad.

> *"If you don't know where you are going, you might wind up someplace else."*
>
> –Yogi Berra

CHAPTER 3

Live In The Present.
The Good Ole Days Aren't So Good.

Live in the here and now. Forget yesterday, but not God. Move forward as He wills and directs. Solomon wrote,

Proverbs 3:5-6, MSG – *"Trust God from the bottom of your heart; don't try to figure out everything on your own. Listen for God's voice in everything you do, everywhere you go; He's the one who will keep you on track. Don't assume that you know it all. Run to God! Run from evil!"*

That's not only good advice, it is Good News at any age. Trust God and live, *"not on your own understanding,"* which is never terribly perceptive or discerning (to say the least), but rather on His written word, precepts, and divine instructions and commands. Forget yesterday and start living today in light of God's life-giving principles that *"restores the soul ... makes wise the simple ... rejoices the "heart ... (and) enlightens the eyes' (Psalm 19:7-8).* A sure approach to Christian living that gets results, saving a lot of heartache, lessens poor decisions, and avoids a host of regrets. Looking back to yesteryear when you lived apart from God and yearning for days gone by will surely put an end to the advancement of your personal life, kill your hopes and dreams, your current relationships, and destroy your resolve to experience life on a higher plane as God intended. Wanting to go back to "Egypt" (Numbers 14:3-4) is a killer.

Where I am, where I'm going, and how I will get there by the close of my life story is of utmost importance and critical to my continued psychological, emotional, and physical well-being,[23] and I might add, my spiritual health. A reset in my thinking must take place, especially as I get older.

When Jesus first called Peter, He basically told him to forget his past failures. He had fished all night and caught nothing. That was yesterday, where an unworthy, *"sinful man"* goes. Christ responded with a new set of instructions. He said, *"Put out into the deep water and let down your nets for a catch"* (Luke 5:4). Peter and the others did just that, and their lives dramatically changed forever. They *"left everything (boats, nets, livelihood, etc.) and followed Him"* (Luke 5:11). A number of life lessons emerge from the story that helps to keep me focused on the promise of today and tomorrow and not the failures and sins of my past.

- My past is no indication of what I can become in the future.
- Sin sees what I am and where I've been. God sees what I can be and where I can go.
- Jesus sees more in me than my sin permits me to see in myself.

---

[23] Danan Gu, Bethany L. Brown, and LiQui, *Self-perceived uselessness is associated with lower likelihood of successful aging among older adults in China,* BMC Geriatrics.

- I see the problems that will hold me back in my life, but Christ sees the potential *for* my life.

Live in the present with hope for tomorrow, which is where God works best. Let yesterday go. Look forward, and see what God can do.

What God calls a man who is a murderer and then later raises up that same man to liberate a nation from slavery? What God anoints a snotty, young, inexperienced boy, who spent most of his growing up years talking with sheep only to become a king? What God uses a harlot to help an army bring down the walls of a mighty city, or empowers a dirty, crusty old fisherman with a mouth on him to kick down the very gates of Hell? What God takes defective, malfunctioning, imperfect, fallen human beings (I'm a card-carrying member of that club), and lifts them to their feet, cleans them up, and then sends them out in His name to change the world for the better? None of it makes any sense. From a human perspective, none of it seems reasonable, rational, prudent, or wise. None of these individuals would pass a background check for IBM let alone work in the kingdom of a holy God! None of the disciples would be employable by conventional standards.

But Let God be God. He does the unexpected. He has his own agenda and His own way of doing things and the means to accomplish His will in this world and in my life. His way is best. His plan is perfect—an ongoing, never-ending process that continues throughout the universe and at every stage of life.

D.L. Moody (1837-1899), spent nearly half a century preaching the good news of Christ to millions. He had but "one aim in life…to do the will of God." Not bad for a shoe salesman. His son wrote of his father that his entire life was characterized by a "readiness to God's summons" right up to the very end of his days. He never wavered. He lived an active life for sixty-two years, mostly illness free. As his heart weakened and his strength subsided, he needed complete rest. During his last few days, Moody said, "I'm not discouraged. There's lots of hard work left in me yet, I believe. I want to live as long as I'm useful (to God and His kingdom), but when my work is done I want to be up and off."[24] Me, too. Moody died a few days later, December 22, 1899. His mission was complete. His joy, full. His eternal future, secured. His soul at peace. He never looked back. Neither should we.

To the believers at Phillipi, Paul wrote, *"I forget what was before and press forward to the call of God in Christ Jesus"* (Philippians 3:12). We would be smart to follow his lead. It was never his intention to return to his former life, though he wielded enormous power and success as a *"persecutor"* of first century Christians (Philippians 3:6) and a staunch, ruthless defender of the Laws of Judaism. He held a position of high rank among Jewish sympathizers and enjoyed the prestige of social and religious standing— an educated, respected man among his peers with the equivalent of a PhD in Theology behind his name. He called himself *"a Hebrew of Hebrews...a Pharisee"* (Philippians 3:5). An impressive résumé by most any standard. He oozed *"self-confidence"* (Philippians 3:4) and was full of pride in his personal and professional life, a pedigree among the elite, a chest full of medals. He had every reason to be proud ... until the day the apostle met Jesus on the road to Damascus (Acts 9:3-22). The man was never the same. *"Old things passed away"* (2 Corinthians 5:17). All things became new, especially the man himself. Even his Hebrew name, Saul, was dropped for his Greek name, Paul (see Acts 13:9). He was well known among his peers as an enemy of the Gospel and a blasphemer of the name of Christ. Following his miraculous conversion, the man emerged from the rubble of his own hateful, destructive behavior, as Paul, a *"bond-servant of Christ"*

---

[24] William R. Moody, The Life of Dwight. L. Moody by His Son, (New York, Fleming B. Revell Company, 1900), 351.

(Philippians 1:1), *"an Apostle of Jesus Christ by the will of God"* (Ephesians 1:1, 1 Corinthians 1:1), and *"a follower and proclaimer of God's Son"* (Romans 1:9, 16). The change was extraordinary, unexplainable, supernaturally charged. God's hand was all over his conversion and his life.

The grace and mercy of God could not have been more evident in the man's life. His transformation was miraculous, decisive, and permanent. He could never go back to what he once was ... ever. He wouldn't go back. He shouldn't. Neither should we. Paul was called of God, so are we. His focus was no longer about yesteryear. His full attention was now given over to a godly vision of what he could be (see Acts 9:17-19) in this life. It is where we all must be, including in our closing years. Leave yesterday's successes and failures behind. They don't matter anymore. Here is Paul's testimony:

> **Philippians 3:12-14, NLT** – *"Forgetting the past and looking forward to what lies ahead... I press on to reach the end of the race and receive the heavenly prize for which God, through Christ Jesus, is calling us."*

Things are not always what you remember them to be.

Fifteen days out from Egypt, Israel wanted to go back, ready to quit on God. A ridiculous notion, but an all too familiar story. Moses reminded them, *"By a powerful hand the Lord brought you out from this place"* (see Exodus 13:3, 9, 14, 16). He has done the same for you and me. He has brought us to *"this place"* after many years; through trials and tribulations, through the valleys of tears and heartache, through the dry desert and the barren wastelands of trouble and despair. And sometimes He has taken us to the heights of victory and glory. Through it all, He has never failed us. Four times Moses reminded the people of God's mind-boggling strength, consistent faithfulness, and incredible goodness, but they didn't listen. They simply pulled back and shut down.

In fact, they failed to calculate God into the equation of their daily lives. Instead, they grumbled in the *"wilderness"* (Exodus 13:17-18). I can relate. I have a short memory. I am quick to fear and lean toward skepticism, especially when life is threatening and not working out as I would like. Sometimes faith comes hard. In fact, my tendency is to build an entire theology based on what God *didn't* do for me when I asked Him. I suspect you struggle with a similar malady, looking to either redefine the character of God (He's not good), or at the very least, put Him back on the shelf to collect dust. At some point, we are all too ready to head back to recapture our former days and live apart from God as slaves—slaves to our appetites, subservient to our emotions, and worried and confused in our thinking, if we are thinking at all.

Israel stood on the banks of the Red Sea and saw in the distance Egypt's war machine closing in for the kill. They feared for their lives and wrongly assessed their current situation as helpless, hopeless, and hapless. They screamed at Moses, *"Leave us alone that we may serve the Egyptians than to die in the wilderness"* (Exodus 14:12). They were fully aware of the might, ferociousness, and brutality of Pharoah's army. They had seen them in action before. Not surprisingly, their thoughts quickly returned to the "good ole days" back in Egypt where life seemed somewhat more predictable. Maybe so, but in those moments of panic, slavery seemed more attractive than simply trusting God who had proven Himself time and time again (as He has done in our own lives) to be faithful and capable of securing their future and remedying their problems.

Ten times God supernaturally brought Egypt to its knees and reminded the people that God is King over all, not Pharaoh. The plagues (the boils, the hail, the locust, etc.) that struck Egypt served to highlight the person and power of God and His personal involvement and investment in His people.

The last plague was particularly effective. Every first born in the land, including the cattle, not covered by the *"blood of the lamb"* on the door post of a home, died that night when the angel of death moved across the land of pagan Egypt. When the sun rose the next day, there was no doubt who was in charge. God was on His throne, and nothing could thwart His advancement nor alter His objectives and plans. *"No word from God shall be void of power; nothing will be impossible with God"* (Luke 1:37). God was on the move, and Israel missed it. They lost sight of the presence of God Almighty and its implications for their lives going forward. Unfortunately, they wanted to return to Egyptian soil to live again under the yoke of the taskmaster's whip, thinking that yesterday was better with the Egyptians than their future with God. Foolish people! Careful now. You may have thought the same way. I have.

They had forgotten the *"hard labor"* (Exodus 1:11) pressed upon them, the sting of the lash, the loss of control over their daily affairs. Slavery was a life of large-scale, coerced labor at the hands of taskmasters and the elite, ruling parties of Egypt. The people of God were treated as property, a commodity bought and sold in the slave markets of the great cities. *"And the Egyptians compelled the sons of Israel to labor rigorously; and they made their lives bitter…"* (Exodus 1:13-14). All slaves were branded. Their children were born into slavery.[25] Slaves were harshly punished for disobedience. The Pharaohs held the lives of the sons and daughters of Israel in the palms of their hands. They determined who would live and who would die (Exodus 1:16, 22). Infant males were slaughtered. Females were spared for a life of servitude. A slave's life was no life at all. It was highly restrictive, unduly bleak, inhuman, and thoroughly hopeless. Their lives were not their own,

---

[25] Karev, E. (2023). Ancient Egyptian Slavery. In: Pargas, D.A., Schiel, J. (eds) The Palgrave Handbook of Global Slavery throughout History. Palgrave Macmillan, Cham. https://doi.org/10.1007/978-3-031-13260-5_3, retrieved from https://link.springer.com/chapter/10.1007/978-3-031-13260-5_3.

since they lived at the mercy of slave owners who held the reigns of authority. Slaves had little future or opportunity to speak of—limited prospects beyond the mud pits of Egypt. Yet, they wanted back in. Amazing. Careful, as an old man I might view my past the same way, demanding to return to yesteryear and miss God's best.

For 146,000 days (that's 400 years), the nation lived under mighty Egypt, the power of the ancient world. There was little hope for themselves and for their children. A better tomorrow was just a pipe dream, a passing thought void of substance and reality. It wasn't until God in His time decided to put into motion a rescue plan that would take Israel from slavery to liberty, from despair and dejection to a life of prosperity and great promise. But they settled for much less and were willing to exchange God's person and ageless plans for a fruit salad and some veggies (see Exodus 16:3; Numbers 11:4-6). Read it for yourself. They had forgotten the harsh reality of life under the Egyptian whip. It's not uncommon for flesh and blood to want back the good old days, which ironically weren't ever that good.

When Israel first arrived at the shores of the Jordan, they fell into the same old trap. They wanted out of God's purpose and plans for their lives. Twelve spies were sent into the promised land of Canaan to check things out. Forty days later, they returned with a report, and it wasn't good. The land was better than expected, but the inhabitants were too strong, too big, well-armed, and dug-in behind the large walls of Jericho. A formidable enemy ready for battle, a heavily fortified city, a daunting challenge. Ten spies said, "Don't go. We can't win" (Numbers 13:31). In their own eyes, the people saw themselves as no better or bigger than a bug, *"grasshoppers"* to be more accurate, to be stepped on, squashed, and swatted (Numbers 13:33) down like insects. Israel had no chance of victory if a fight broke out. So they thought. The odds were stacked against them. Their conclusion was final. God was not big enough to deliver on His promises. They would lose the battle and were ready to turn tail and run.

Two spies (Joshua and Caleb) reported something different. Canaan was *"an exceedingly good land"* (Numbers 14:7). The city was theirs for the taking. Victory was assured. They couldn't lose. The day belonged to them for the Lord was with them (Numbers 14:7-9). There was no doubt. No fear. Only a strong, unwavering belief in the word of Almighty God who promised to secure their future. That's something we all could use, a little spiritual moxie.

Unfortunately, the people chose *" (to) appoint a leader and return to Egypt"* (Exodus 14:4). Before them lay God's best, and they turned it down. God put things in perspective. *"How long will this people spurn (treat with contempt, distain, disrespect) Me…and not believe in Me"* (Numbers 14:11)? Unbelief is costly. They lacked faith, and missed God in the process, a high price to pay for their unwillingness to take God at His word. Bad choice.

Yesterday is gone, and yet there stands before us all an abundance of blessing from the hand of God in our old age and beyond. Lean into the Lord God and His ability to deliver on His promises. He was there in your past. Always has been. He is with you today, and He plans to stick around until your body becomes dust and your spirit returns to Him who gave it life (Ecclesiastes 12:7).

Elizabeth Elliot wrote in her book, *Keep A Quiet Heart*,

> *Once we give ourselves (young or old) up to God, shall we attempt to get hold of what can never belong to us— tomorrow (or my past)? Our lives are His (from start to finish and beyond). Our times are in His hand, He is Lord over what WILL happen, never mind what MAY happen.*[26]

---

[26] Elizabeth Elliot, *Keep A Quiet Heart: A 100 Devotional Readings*, (Ann Arbor, Michigan: Servant Publications, 1996), 53.

Run, don't walk, to the *"Prince of Peace,"* the One Who is called, *"Wonderful Counselor, Mighty God, Eternal Father,"* (Isaiah 9:6, KJV), the sovereign God of the universe Who loves you and rules and reigns over the affairs of your daily life. Life may become chaotic and scary, and the future may seem bleak and uncertain. You may feel useless, confused, and out of sync, and that life has somehow passed you by. You've nothing more to give, or so you think. Yet our times remain in His strong hands now and forever.

Paul Flemming is the main character in Henry W. Longfellow's novel, *Hyperion: A Romance*. As the story unfolds, Paul walks into a "little chapel" and stumbles upon an inscription written on a funeral tablet hanging on the wall. He read the few short lines, then "bowed his stubborn knees, and wept." It simply read:

> *Look not mournfully into the past. It comes not back again. Wisely improve the present. It is thine. Go forth to meet the shadowy future, without fear, and with a manly heart.*[27]

Good advice for old folk. Improve the present. Live out the remainder of your life with courage and face the months and years ahead with an obedient heart to make the most of the days you've got left.

As long as there is breath in our bodies, life can happen. It must happen. Who wants to go back when better days are on the horizon? Certainly, not me. The end is approaching fast. Heaven and an eternity to enjoy the presence of God forever awaits. Our most productive years may yet lay before us.

Psalm 77, composed by Asaph, is a song about a man who was in *"deep trouble"* (v. 2). The lyrics sound a bit country-western, if you ask me. We're not exactly sure what he was facing. We are not

---

[27] Henry W. Longfellow, *Hyperion: A Romance*, Project Gutenberg eBook, Book 4, Chapter 8, 1839, retrieved from
https://www.gutenberg.org/cache/epub/5436/pg5436-images.html

told, but it was apparently quite significant. He is seen crying, tears are flowing. Sleep has escaped him, and he is unable to pray (been there, done that)—plagued with sorrow, mournful complaining, disappointed and dissatisfied with the present, and uncertain about tomorrow. Emotionally, the man was suffering terribly, wanting to turn back the clock to the past. That's neither helpful nor productive. We get a little glimpse into how he first handled his grief and turmoil.

> **Psalm 77: 5-7, NLT** – *"I think of the good old days, long since ended, when my nights were filled with joyful songs. I search my soul and ponder the difference now. Has the Lord rejected me forever? Will he never again be kind to me?"*

The psalmist is stuck in the past, like so many— unable to move forward and wanting to go back to a day and time when life seemed more appealing, more pleasant. It didn't help him much. It never does. There is nothing there of any substance. No answers. No lasting joy. No clear picture of reality, just a shadow of what once was. Any one of us could have written the words of that Psalm. There is, however, a remedy.

One hundred-plus years ago, hymn writer Johnson Oatman gave an important recommendation for living life at any age from youth to seniors. He wrote, "Count Your Blessings."[28] Simple, profound, instructive words.

My sister has Alzheimer's. Her thoughts are now jumbled. Her memory is fading. Her emotions are unstable. Her personality is changing. A shadow of the woman she once was. But the one thing she clearly remembers are the words of her favorite song, which never were lost to her heart and mind. To this day, at 78 years old, weakened by a dreadful, cruel disease, she sings with great conviction, "Count your blessings, name them one by one; Count

---

[28] Johnson Oatman, Jr., *Count Your Blessings,* (Public Domain, 1897).

your many blessings, see what God has done." I can still hear her singing and telling me how that wonderful hymn had carried her through many a dark day. It still does, and she is still singing. I feel dwarfed in the presence of such raw wisdom and child-like love for the God who comforts the soul, soothes an anxious spirit, and gives strength to a weaken heart.

Do likewise. Remember the Lord and all that God has accomplished in the past throughout your lifetime and mine. Don't forget His goodness when hell seems to have broken loose. Remember His mercy for the forgiveness of our sins and the rebellious nature of our hearts. Recall His gracious offer to freely give us the gift of eternal life and the riches of heaven in Christ Jesus that await. Don't forget about His compassion that mends broken hearts (including yours and mine), His guidance when we've lost our way, His faithfulness not to quit on us, His wisdom that shows us the only way to live, His love to embrace us when no one else will, His grace to sustain us through all of life's ups and downs, and His strength and power to lift us out of the pit of despair and hopelessness, get us up on our feet, brush off the dirt, and enable us to live life for the better.

Take a spiritual inventory. Indeed, count your blessings, and give thanks to the Lord. Remember all *"of His benefits"* (see Psalm 103:1-14) for your life—the very breath in my body, the home I live in, the food on my table (especially Italian sausage, meatballs, and angel-hair spaghetti), the "chariot" I own and ride every day, the job and career I've worked to support my family, the medicine that relieves my pain and the antibiotics that heal my diseases, and finally, the laughter I enjoy, the people I've met, and the experiences I've had (all of them, the good and the not so good). God has permitted them all to make me the man I am today, a better man than I was yesterday. Though some days have been tough and hard on this journey, I know that there would be no days at all if it wasn't for God who rules and regulates my life.

That focus alters one's thinking and ultimately behavior. It changes a person's entire demeanor. The Psalmist looked at the totality of his life, past, present, and future, and used it all as a reminder of the very provision of God throughout his daily life, every minute of every day. Consequently, he stopped his self-pity and refocused his spiritual eyes, if you will, on the divine *"cloud by day,"* and the *"fire by night,"* which providentially guided a bunch of liberated slaves out of Egypt to the promised land. God *"never left"* them. He *"went ahead of them"* (Exodus 13:21-22, MSG). His strong arms comforted them yesterday. He'll do it again today. Yesterday His word brought security and stability to their lives. Today His word will again be an anchor to their souls and ours. That is the assurance of the presence and providence of God throughout the ages, at every stage of life. What real comfort and encouragement! Asaph sang:

> **Psalm 77:11-12, NLT** – *"But then I recall all you have done, O Lord; I remember your wonderful deeds of long ago. They are constantly in my thoughts. I cannot stop thinking about your mighty* works."

His perspective changed. It needed to. So does mine. His attention turned to God, and it worked. It always does. There is no excuse for a grumpy old man.

G. Campbell Morgan (1863-1945), the British evangelist, author, and Bible teacher of another generation, commented on Psalm 77:

> *The message of the psalm is that to brood on sorrow is to be broken and disheartened, while to see God is to sing on the darkest day. Once we come to know that our years are of His right hand, there is light everywhere...*[29]

---

[29] G. Campbell Morgan, *An Exposition of the Whole Bible*, (Old Tappan, New Jersey: Fleming H. Revell Company, 1959), 249.

The God-adventure is not over, even when I've breathed my last on planet Earth and lowered into the ground. The last chapter has not yet been written. I can still move forward in some capacity well into my "golden" years. What God did in former times with amazing wisdom and unbridled goodness is but a foretaste of what He is able to do today and what He promises to do tomorrow in and through my life. God still commands and orders my daily steps. God still has use of me in His great cause. God is still able to strengthen me for kingdom service here in this world and help me to remain faithful to His will for my life until the inevitable end. That is a much better approach to living out our last few days or years.

Mother Teresa died at eighty-seven years old on September 5, 1997. She had spent the better portion of her life working tirelessly to serve the poor, care for the sick, and help the destitute and the homeless of Calcutta. That was her heart. That was her divine mission—to bring the love and hope of God to the streets where people suffered and died daily. She did it for nearly fifty years as the founder and head of the Missionaries of Charity. Her last words as she was dying reflect the focus of her entire life right up to the end. She whispered, "Jesus, I love you. Jesus, I offer myself to you. My God, I thank you, praise you, and adore you. Jesus, I love you."[30] She died without the riches of this world. She had no barns in which to stockpile her wealth. No bank accounts. No stock options. No retirement funds. Just a deep love for God and people exhibited in the life she lived. She died a selfless, servant-oriented, generous woman with a heart for the wounded of this world. Her greatest treasures were the souls she touched throughout her lifetime. She

---

[30] SA Editor, A Conversation with Mother Teresa, *Scrupulous Anonymous*, Sept 1, 2023, retrieved from https://scrupulousanonymous.org/2023/09/01/a-conversation-with-mother-teresa/#:~:text=On%20September%205%2C%201997%2C%20the,Jesus%2C%20I%20love%20you.%E2%80%9D

was a person who lived a life of immeasurable value to the God she served and the people she loved, right up to the end of her days.

Now, I'm no Mother Teresa, but I can live daily and deliberately and make a difference ministering the love and mercy of God to the people I rub shoulders with every day, wherever I am, at whatever age, young or old. There is no better way to close out one's life—in ministry, in service to King Jesus. Forget yesterday. Tackle today. Look ahead.

"You only live once, but if you do it right, once is enough."

–Mae West (1893-1980), American actress, singer, and playwright

CHAPTER 4

Avoid Living On Yesterday's Headlines. You Still Have Something Left To Give Today.

I recall the first day of my retirement. I got up early, had a cup of coffee, ate some breakfast, watched the local news and weather, and then walked down the hallway to my office. I then closed the door and hung the "Do Not Disturb" sign. I wanted to be alone, just me and God to talk without interruption. I sat at my desk, and for a moment, looked around at the shelves of books that represented years of study and teaching. I sighed, hardly believing it had all finally ended abruptly. Fifty years of ministry flashed before my eyes. It was over. At least, that's what I thought. Where had it all gone? Me and God needed to talk. I remember my words in the first hours of retirement like it was yesterday. I thought to myself,

> *You're not done yet, boy. God is not through with you. Get a new vision and do it quickly. Make new memories. Explore new paths. New adventures. New ministries. Get out of the rut. Do what you can do today. You may not get another chance. God will take care of tomorrow. You,*

however, get on with today. Yesterday no longer really counts.

Then I prayed,

Lord, as You maintain my health, I will continue to serve You and Your kingdom with everything I can muster until the day you call me home. I do not plan to sit around this house, do nothing of any consequence, and wait to die. That's not for me. I will find something productive to do with my life that is worth my time and effort and the glory of Your name. I will not whittle away whatever years You have afforded me. Whatever time I've got left, I want to use it as You see fit. For as long as there is breath in my body, direct me and show me new opportunities for ministry. Lord, let me covenant with You to serve Your kingdom. "Here I am. Send me" (Isaiah 6:8).

How we live our lives, the decisions we make, the roads we take, the places we go, the pursuits of our heart matter greatly. Life marches on ... no matter what. The sun comes up in the eastern sky every morning and sets in the west like clockwork. A 24-hour day is predictable until God decides to bring the curtain down on this world. It is the same for all of creation.

In honor of the twenty-seventh anniversary of Jim Valvano's death, *Sports Illustrated* published his entire speech given at the ESPY Awards, March 4, 1993. That was a special night. In those few moments, a man dying of cancer stood to share his heart and encourage the rest of us, young and old alike, in our journey toward the finish line. Here is in part what he said:

I have some things that I would like to say ... I always have to think about what's important in life ... Where you started, where you are, and where you're going to be.

When people say to me how do you get through life or each day, it's the same thing ... laugh ... think ... cry, that's a full day.

I think you have to have an enthusiasm for life. You have to have a dream, a goal. You have to be willing to work for it ...(and) enjoy your life, the precious moments you have ... keep your dreams alive in spite of problems whatever you have ... don't ever give up. And that's what I'm going to try to do every minute that I have left. I will thank God for the day and the moment I have... I'd like to think, I'm going to fight my brains out to be back here again next year.[31]

Less than two months later, Jimmy Valvano died on April 28, 1993, at just 47 years old. By all accounts, a young man. Before he left this world, he gave birth to the Jimmy V Foundation for Cancer Research which has carried forward its mission and Valvano's motto, "Don't give up... don't ever give up." Words to live by at any age. He could have rested on an NCAA Division 1 National Collegiate Basketball Championship coaching his underdog North Carolina State team to victory in 1983, a great accomplishment in the world of sports. An unexpected win, considered by some as "a huge upset" over the number one team, the Houston Cougars. No one saw it coming. Forty-two years have passed since that night, and I can still picture a young 37 year-old Valvano running out onto the court wildly waving his arms, looking for someone, anyone, to hug and celebrate the final whistle of a hard-fought championship. Ten years later he lost a ten-month battle with cancer. Atlantic Coast Conference commissioner, Gene Corrigan, said of Valvano, "He put up a good fight. It's amazing what a constitution he had. I don't know how many of us could have done what he did."[32]

---

[31] Brett Friedlander, Jimmy V's 'Don't Ever Give Up' Speech, *Sports Illustrated*, April 28, 2020, retrieved from
https://www.si.com/college/ncstate/basketball/jimmy-v-espy-speech.

[32] Don Markus, Valvano loses fight with cancer : College basketball: respected but embattled, the former coach and commentator dies at 47 after a 10-month battle, Los Angeles Times, April 30, 1993, retrieved from
https://www.latimes.com/archives/la-xpm-1993-04-30-sp-29411-story.html.

That's how I want to go out, having "put up a good fight." Not whittling away the opportunities given to me by God to achieve what few have ever done. I'm not interested in resting on yesterday's headlines, good or bad. I want to keep moving forward until the final whistle. So should you.

The great opera composer George Frideric Handel died the day before Easter 1749. He was 56 years old. Before his death, he suffered from bankruptcy on two separate occasions, physical pain, depression, and discouragement. He and his work had become objects of scorn and rejection by the social elite crowd and church contemporaries. Once he was called a "German nincompoop." Thinking his career was over, Handel scheduled his farewell performance in London in the spring of 1741. However, that summer this "nincompoop" composed *Messiah,* 260 pages of musical score in just twenty-four days, a remarkable accomplishment. *Messiah* was considered the "epitome of the Christian faith." He said of the *Hallelujah Chorus*, "I did think I did see all Heaven before me, and the great God himself."[33] Following his death, a close friend remarked of Handel, "He died as he lived—a good Christian, with a true sense of his duty to God and to man." That's how I want to be remembered. That's how I want the final assessment of my life to read—"a Christian, who fulfilled his duty to God and to man." Paul wrote a summary of daily, Christian living:

> **Galatians 6:9-10, NLT** – *"So let's not get tired of doing what is good. At just the right time we will reap a harvest of blessing if we don't give up. Therefore, whenever we have the opportunity, we should do good to everyone— especially to those in the family of faith."*

Former Emperor of Rome and Stoic Philosopher, Marcus Aurelius (161-180 AD) suggested that you and I should "live each

---

[33] Christian History Magazine Editorial Staff. 131 Christians Everyone Should Know (Holman Reference) (p. 112). B&H Publishing Group. Kindle Edition.

day as if it were your last because tomorrow may never come." An admonition we might very well consider, a charge to every man or woman who ever wore a toga or a pair Calvin Klein designer jeans, the rags of a pauper, or the latest in hospital gown fashion—to live thoughtfully, intentionally, focused on what's truly important, vital, and of great value while you can. You may not get another chance. Keep your priorities straight. Hold on to what's true. Discard everything else. Make new "headlines."

Go thou and do likewise …

There is nothing – no circumstance, no trouble, no testing – that can ever touch me until, first of all, it has gone past God and past Christ right through to me. If it has come that far, it has come with a great purpose, which I may not understand at the moment. But as I refuse to become panicky, as I lift up my eyes to Him and accept it as coming from the throne of God for some great purpose of blessing to my own heart, no sorrow will ever disturb me, no trial will ever disarm me, no circumstance will cause me to fret – for I shall rest in the joy of what my Lord is! That is the rest of victory![34]

–Alan Redpath

CHAPTER 5

Lean on God. There Is Nothing, Absolutely Nothing, You Can't Trust Him With

The entire Bible from cover to cover is filled with references and stories regarding the necessity of living daily in faith and trust in God. To live *"by faith and not by sight"* is at the core of Christianity. Paul wrote,

> **2 Corinthians 5:7, AMPC** – *"For we walk by faith [we regulate our lives and conduct ourselves by our*

---

[34] Bill Muehlenberg, Notable Christians: Alan Redpath, *Culture Watch*, November 5, 2022, retrieved from https://billmuehlenberg.com/2022/11/05/notable-christians-alan-redpath/.

conviction or belief...with trust and holy fervor; thus we walk] not by sight or appearance."

The terms faith (action), trust (assurance/reliable), and hope (expectations) are nearly synonymous concepts with slight variations. As a whole, they carry a sense of assurance, reliability, trustworthiness, confidence, fidelity, conviction, belief, and certainty. The words are used in classical Greek to describe persons and personal conduct, marital contracts, and those bound by treaty. The concept of obedience must also be included in any discussion of genuine faith (see Romans 1:5, 16:26) and centered on man's positive response to God, who is the object of our faith and trust.[35]

To trust God is to know the character of God, as revealed in the Scriptures. The revelation of God (the truth about God) becomes the firm foundation upon which our faith/trust/hope rests. I depend on God's ability, strength, love, promises, wisdom, and goodness to always do the right thing by me and for me. His decisions are always for my benefit, though admittedly they often remain beyond my comprehension to fully grasp their implications for my life.

We must not become men and women *"of little faith"* (Matthew 17:20), living with little trust, and *"no hope"* (1 Thessalonians 4:13), living as if God does not exist, or God is not interested or involved in my personal life. He is. His intent has always been to raise me up to live a better life well beyond what I might "normally expect or anticipate" (see John 10:10, NET footnote b). God will never do me harm. He applies and extends His infinite love, His moment-by-moment, unending care and immeasurable mercy until the very close of my life. His presence and providence, His lovingkindness and thoughts have always pursued me. God is an extraordinary hunter. He tracks me until He

---

[35] G. Kittel, G. W. Bromiley, & G. Friedrich (Eds.), *Theological Dictionary of the New Testament* (electronic ed., Vol. 6, p. 176). Eerdmans.

finds me, like the man who leaves his ninety-nine sheep to search for the one that was lost (Luke 15:3-7). Let the "rejoicing" begin.

In writing for Proverbs 31 Ministries, Abby McDonald wrote in her devotional: "Here's what blows my mind: Each promise God has made in the Bible, from Genesis through Revelation, is motivated by one desire — His longing to be with you and me.[36] It blows my mind, too, when I consider just how faithful God is and the lengths He would go to have a relationship with the likes of me.

Francis Thompson (1859-1907) was destitute and addicted to opium. He wandered through the streets of London, homeless and alone, an utterly hopeless human being. He wrote an autobiographical poem entitled "The Hound of Heaven" (1890), the story of his redemption and the God who relentlessly tracked him down and would not quit until He captured the man's heart. He redeemed his life from the pit and *crown*ed (him) with lovingkindness and compassion (see Psalm 103:4). God just doesn't quit.

> *I fled Him, down the nights and down the days;*
> *I fled Him, down the arches of the years;*
> *I fled Him, down the labyrinthine ways*
> *Of my own mind; and in the midst of tears*
> *I hid from Him, and under running laughter.*
> *Up vistaed hopes I sped ...*
> *From those strong Feet that followed, followed after.*
> *But with unhurrying chase,*
> *And unperturbèd pace,*
> *Deliberate speed, majestic instancy,*
> *They beat—and a Voice beat*

---

[36] Abby McDonald, When you long for certainty in the road ahead, *Encouragement for Today Devotions, Proverbs 31 Ministries,* May 14, 2025, retrieved from devotions@proverbs31.org.

More instant than the Feet—
'All things betray thee, who betrayest Me'.[37]

The story of Nicki Cruz, former NYC gang leader, is a testament to the love, grace, and persistence of God. At the age of fifteen, Cruz became a gang member and eventually the leader of the Mau Mau's, a violent gang, fighting his way through the streets of New York, drinking hard, and selling and using drugs, etc., a destructive life style, guaranteed to end in an early grave. But a man by the name of David Wilkerson "fell from heaven" with the message of the cross, a message about the love, mercy, and grace of God. "God became my last hope" Cruz said, "and in my misery He found me." Like a "wild animal, Cruz beat and brutalized Wilkerson before three hundred witnesses. He hit him, cursed him, grabbed his hair, and banged his head against a wall. Bruised and bleeding, amidst the pain, Wilkerson quietly said to his assailant, "Nicky, I'm not scared. I came here to bring you the news from heaven. I came to tell you, Nikki, Jesus loves you! " The beating stopped. Cruz stared at him in unbelief at what he just heard.

"If you want, you can kill me. And I know you can. But even if you kill me and cut me into a thousand pieces and spread them across the street, remember: every piece will scream to you. Nicki, Jesus loves you!"

Later, Cruz admitted, "I saw Jesus Christ crucified before my eyes, so alive that I thought I was there, and saw Him die. And this touched me deeply. I was defeated by Jesus' perseverance." The Hound of Heaven.

God's love never fails. His faithfulness and mercy never cease (Lamentations 3:22-23). You can trust God throughout your life. He is faithful to the very end of your days and mine.

---

[37] Francis Thompson, The Hound of Heaven, *Catholicism*, Eternal Word Television Network, no date, retrieved from https://www.ewtn.com/catholicism/library/hound-of-heaven-4117.

The Hebrew word translated *"follow"* found in the 23rd Psalm is simply not strong enough to express the aggressive nature, activity, and work of God in my life. His *"goodness and lovingkindness"* (v. 6) pursue me wherever I go with an unrelenting, ruthless resolve. He has stood at my side before the foundations of the world were ever laid, at my right hand and my left. He goes before me and behind me. He has never let me down. He has remained faithful and trustworthy during the course of my eighty years. I expect Him to continue to do so on into eternity.

I believe Him. I believe He loves me. He knows my frame. He knows my name (see Isaiah 43:1-4, MSG). I am His, *"bought with a price"* (1 Corinthians 6:20), His adopted son *"according to His good pleasure"* (Ephesians 1:5). Like a good Father, a good Shepherd, a good Protector, a good Provider, and a good Counselor, He will make straight my path and keep me on track (see Proverbs 3:5-6). The saints of every age and generation bear witness to His trustworthiness, plain and simple. God will do as God does. He will, in fact, never change. A.W. Tozer wrote in his classic, *The Knowledge of the Holy*,

> *God being who He is, cannot cease to be what He is, and being what He is, He cannot act out of character with Himself. He is at once faithful and immutable, so all His words and acts must be and remain faithful.*[38]

His Word, God's message to the world, stands firm forever, as He speaks into my life.

God will come through for you and me. I can rely on Him and lean on Him to reach me right where I am, amid my greatest need, racked with physical pain, or loaded with guilt, shame, character flaws, an abundance of weaknesses, and personal failures. When I fall, He picks me up, dusts me off, and takes a firm hold of my life until the day I walk through the gates of eternity and heaven. I'll

---

[38] Tozer, AW; Editors, GP. *The Knowledge of the Holy: The Attributes of God* (AW Tozer Series Book 2), GENERAL PRESS. Kindle Edition, 38.

always be thankful that God in His mercy and grace took notice of an unfaithful, arrogant, self-serving, dysfunctional man with a lengthy list of offenses against God and men alike. Yet, God refuses not to love me.[39]

I believe in a hill called Golgotha, where *The Old Rugged Cross*[40] of Christ took care of my past. He said it would. I believe Him. It did. I believe that the resurrection of Christ took charge of my future. He said it would. I accept it, believe it, live it. I have staked everything on Christ, especially the eternal state of my soul. I am fully dependent on God's grace, love, and mercy and nothing else. I'm on my way to heaven because He said so, and for no other reason. When there was no way to see myself in the good graces of God, God in Christ became *"the way, the truth, and the life"* (John 14:6)—life today and life tomorrow. To a guilty, dying thief Jesus said, *"I assure you* (there is no doubt or question about it)*, today you will be with me in paradise"* (Luke 23:43, NLT), and he was. His word is good. He is exactly who He said He is, who He was, and who He will always be. He does what He says He will do. Count on it, whether you're young or old, a saint or sinner, rich or poor, educated or not. God never changes. He is always the same. His love is everlasting. It is forever, no matter what may or may not transpire in my life. His Spirit sustains me through thick and thin. His power and mercy will bring me home to the glories and riches of heaven. My inheritance, *"which is imperishable and undefiled and will not fade away, reserved in heaven"* (1 Peter 1:4) awaits me and you. It is safe, protected, and preserved in eternity. God said so. Therefore, it is. No question.

Quaker, lay speaker, and author, Hannah Whitall Smith (1832-1911), posed some very pointed questions. She asked,

---

[39] Christian Broadcasting Network, February 28, 2025. In an interview with author, speaker, and revivalist, Robert Hotchkin.
[40] George Bennard, *The Old Rugged Cross,* Public Domain, 1913.

> *Why should the children of God lead such utterly, uncomfortable religious lives, when He has led us to believe that His yoke would be easy and His burden light ... why are we tormented with so many spiritual doubts? Why do we find it so hard to be sure that God really loves us, and why is it that we never seem able to believe long at a time in His kindness and care? How is it that we can let us suspect Him of forgetting us and forsaking us in time of need? Does the fault of this state of things lie with the Lord? Has He promised more than He is able to supply? Has He played us false?*[41]

She has an answer. "We have under believed and under trusted (a common practice) ... It is our ignorance of God that does it all. Because we do not know Him..."[42] Timely. Probing. Truthful.

Faith is not blind. Faith is not irrational, irresponsible, unreasonable, baseless, or arbitrary. On the contrary, faith is built and exercised based on the sure revelation of the person of God almighty. *"So faith comes by hearing [what is told], and what is heard comes by the preaching [of the message that came from the lips] of Christ (the Messiah Himself)"* (Romans 10:17, PHILLIPS). Faith brings the reality of God and all His attributes to bear on our lives wherever we may be, whatever situation we are in, and whatever age we might be.

Life may get pretty challenging in your old age. Everything (body, mind, and spirit) seems to wear out or wear down, which is reason enough to live out our days in the closest relationship possible with God, especially in the face of aging and great difficulties it can bring. We need to know and experience God better. King David wrote of courageous faith, which must play a significant role in our lives as we grow older:

---

[41] Hannah Whitall Smith, *God of All Comfort,* (Chicago, Illinois: Moody, 1956), 7.
[42] Ibid, 11.

Psalm 27:1, 14, NKJV – *"The Lord is my light and my salvation; whom shall I fear? The Lord is the strength of my life; of whom shall I be afraid? ... Wait on the Lord: be of good courage, and he shall strengthen thine heart: wait, I say, on the Lord."*

The necessity to trust the Lord every minute of every day to handle life's ups and downs is the key to successful Christian living. One's faith is as strong as the object upon which it rests, a principle best learned in our youth and carried down the road as the end of our days draws near. There is nothing me and God can't handle.

David stood toe-to-toe with a fierce giant named Goliath. The Scriptures record that when he heard the taunting of the giant, David ran to the battle (1 Samuel 17:49) with sling and stones in hand to meet the challenge and silence the arrogance of a man who would dare to mock God. That's significant. Faith demands courage and confidence to face what is seemingly impossible. David had both. *"The God, who delivered me from the teeth of the lion and the claws of the bear, will deliver me from this Philistine* (1 Samuel 17: 37, MSG). Fearless. Gutsy. Dependent on the God Who had come through for him again and again. This time would be no different. David had tested God's faithfulness and character and found God to be true. There in those fields shepherding his father's flocks a young boy learned to trust the person and power of God and concluded that the fierceness of lions and the strength of bears were no match for God and God's man. David learned to walk by faith and not by sight (2 Corinthians 5:7 NIV) and discovered that it was better to avoid looking at the bigness of his problems, and focus more on the bigness and faithfulness of his God.

God was with David during those early days, as He has been with you. God sat with him on cold dark nights, listened to his prayers, his dreams, his heart, comforted him when he was alone, and filled him with strength and courage to do his job, protect the sheep, and face the threat of wild beasts head on. It was this God

Who brought him to the battlefield well prepared for the trials he would face. In the end, David took the head of a giant. You know the story, a story that can be yours and mine. It should be. David's trust and faith in God, learned in his earlier years, carried him through to victory against all odds. "Faith is the victory that overcomes the world."[43] A truth that will sustain you in the closing years of your life. C.H. Spurgeon wrote:

> *No faith is so precious as that which lives and triumphs through adversity. Tested faith brings experience. You would never have believed your own weakness had you not needed to pass through trials. And you would never have known God's strength had His strength not been needed to carry you through.*[44]

Surely, God knows how to build your faith.

Maybe the greatest words of faith ever uttered by flesh and blood belong to Job, a man *who "was honest inside and out, a man of his word, who was totally devoted to God and hated evil with a passion"* (Job 1:1, MSG). A quality man. A successful man. A spiritual man who lived out his days with personall integrity and faithfulness to God. He did so amidst heartbreaking personal tragedy. He was unquestionably a man of faith, but not immune to the problems, setbacks, and tears of life in a fallen world. Nobody is. Job lost everything: possessions, property, position, provisions, etc. Everything he knew was gone. Everything close to him was destroyed. Anything of real human value and importance was ripped from his hands. Old people are all too familiar with that scene. Death unmercifully pounded on his front door. He soon stood before the graves of his ten children and wept over his greatest loss. All dead.

---

[43] John Henry Yates, *Faith is the Victory,* Public Domain, 1891.
[44] Emily Maust Wood, 20 powerful quotes of Charles Spurgeon, *Crosswalk,* September 29, 2020, retrieved from
https://www.crosswalk.com/faith/spiritual-life/20-powerful-quotes-from-charles-spurgeon.html.

A man whose eyes have *"grown dim because of grief"* (Job 17:7). *"His days are past ... (his) plans are torn apart ... the wishes of (his) heart"* (Job 17:11), broken and gone. Nothing remained. Yet, he would not *"curse God and die,"* (Job 2:9) though life had become dreadful and tragic. Even his wife pressured him to give up on God. He refused. Stood his ground, and left the outcome of God's plans to God's perfect will.

The decisions and actions of God belong in the vault of divine wisdom. Nobody fully understands what God is up to but God Himself. Job was no exception to the rule. He would argue his case in the courtroom of God and there declare his unwavering commitment and dedication to the God he had served all his life. He said, *"Though He (God) slay me, yet will I trust (hope, wait) in Him"* (Job 13:15, NKJV). Powerful. During disaster and hardship, Job trusted God to do the right thing and render the right judgement concerning his life. A remarkable response. He bet his entire future and left his life in the strong, capable hands of almighty God, who would and will always do right. There is nothing you can't trust God with, including the most difficult of times that often accompany our declining years.

You never really trust God until you stand on the brink of disaster, in deep pain and great suffering, and look to Him for strength, comfort, encouragement, and a little faith to move mountains (see Matthew 17:20). Now, that's the real thing ... where theology meets practice. Then and only then have you truly trusted Him.

John Stam and Elisabeth Scott first met at Moody Bible Institute in 1929 and later married. They started their young lives serving God and sharing the gospel together in China. That was their mission. John wrote, "I have no goal and no desire beyond Him

(Christ)."⁴⁵ During their ministry, the couple was martyred by Chinese protesters. In a letter home dated Christmas Eve 1932, John shared a poem composed by missionary E.H. Hamilton, following the death of his friend Jack Vinson at the hands of rebel soldiers in northern China. It was entitled, *Afraid? Of What?* It is presented below. A powerful insight into dealing with debilitating fear arising from daily trials, service to God, unexpected challenges, and the uncertainties of life and death in a fallen world. *"Fear Not,"* God's affirmation throughout the ages,

To a young, pregnant woman facing the potential of living life as a social outcast, the angel Gabriel said, *"Do not be afraid"* (Luke 1:30). To Gideon, riddled with doubts about God's willingness and power to hold off another attack by the Midianites, the angel of the Lord came to him with this message, *"The Lord is with you ... Go in this your strength"* (Judges 6:12, 14). To Joshua preparing to lead Israel across the Jordan into Canaan, God said, *"Be strong and courageous! Do not tremble or be dismayed, for the Lord your God is with you wherever you go."* He was about 80 years old (about my age).⁴⁶ To the people enslaved in Babylon, God told them *"Do not fear, for I am with you. Do not anxiously look about you, for I am your God. I will strengthen you, surely I will help you ... "* (Isaiah 41:10). A message of hope and a call for courage for young and old alike.

> *Afraid? Of what?*
> *To feel the spirit's glad release?*
> *To pass from pain to perfect peace,*
> *The strife and strain of life to cease?*
> *Afraid? Of that?*

---

[45] Andrew Montonera, By *Life or By Death: The Life and Legacy of John and Betty Stam*, (Chicago, IL: Moody, 2024), 64.

[46] John Calahan, Never thirsty, *Like the Master's Ministry,* no date, retrieved from https://www.neverthirsty.org/bible-qa/qa-archives/question/how-old-was-joshua-when-he-entered-the-promise-land/.

Afraid? Of what?
Afraid to see the Saviour's face,
To hear His welcome, and to trace,
The glory gleam from wounds of grace,
Afraid? Of that?

Afraid? Of what?
A flash – a crash – a pierced heart;
Brief darkness – Light – O Heaven's art! ...
Afraid? Of that? ...

Afraid? Of what?
To enter into Heaven's rest, ...
Afraid? Of that?

Afraid? Of what?
To do by death what life could not –
Baptize with blood a stony plot,
Till souls shall blossom from the spot?
Afraid? Of that?[47]

John's wife Betty put the Christian life in perspective. Upon hearing of others who had also sacrificed their lives to remain "where (God) called them to serve," she wrote these insightful words, "Here in this work (and in all of life), you have to trust everything to God ... and know that He will do exactly what is best, according to His will." [48]

That about sums it up, "unshaken faith" in whatever circumstance you may find yourself. Entrust everything to Him, whether you are young or old. No exclusions. No holdouts. Everything ... whether your body works or not, whether you are lonely or not, in sickness or in health, in poverty or wealth, whether you are a blue-collar laborer or a corporate executive, whether you

---

[47] E.H. Hamilton, Afraid? of What? (1931), Public Domain, retrieved from Randy Alcorn, *Eternal Perspectives Ministries,* December 26, 2014, https://www.epm.org/resources/2014/Dec/26/afraid-what/.
[48] Op.cite, Montonera, 76.

live in a mansion or a nursing home. It doesn't matter. Trust God. There is nothing to fear for, "Great is Thy faithfulness, O God my Father ... "

Then in a vision I saw a new heaven and a new earth. The first heaven and earth had passed away... I saw the Holy City, the New Jerusalem, descending out of the heavenly realm from the presence of God...And from now on he will tabernacle with them as their God. Now God himself will have his home with them— 'God-with-them' will be their God! He will wipe away every tear from their eyes and eliminate death entirely. No one will mourn or weep any longer. The pain of wounds will no longer exist, for the old order has ceased." And God-Enthroned spoke to me and said, "Consider this! I am making everything to be new and fresh. Write down at once all that I have told you, because each word is trustworthy and dependable."

–Revelations 21:1-5, TPT

Chapter 6

Set Your Eyes Toward Heaven. There Is More To Come.

On a recent episode of The Howard Stern Show (Yes. I said Howard Stern), the "shock-jock" host, asked his guest, music legend Paul Simon, the following questions:

Paul, just give me one last answer. You seem very wise. You've lived through everything. You've created great masterpieces. Is there a God? Because I need to know. I'm getting older. Is this it for me? Am I going to die and that's it, or am I going somewhere? And please answer it in a serious manner.

Great questions. Simon answered,

This is my feeling about God or Creator. The planet that I'm living on is so beautiful and the universe is so awe-inspiring. If that is the work of a creator, I say, "Thanks so much…" If it turns out that there's another explanation for creation, I'm still unbelievably grateful for my existence… (either way) it doesn't matter to me.

It should matter. The answer to the questions, *"Is there a God?" "Am I going to die?" "Is that it?"* will determine the foundation upon which a man will build his life and future.

Stern responded, "But it's so cruel. We have this existence and then we have to disappear. It's hard."[49] Of course, it's hard, living a life that is going nowhere. Spinning our wheels. No direction to speak of. No traction to keep us on course. At best, such living is limited, shortsighted, and lacks any significant punch. A worldview of "nothing." No purpose. No meaning. No hope. Who wants it? Who needs it? Not me.

Matthew Perry starred in the sitcom *Friends,* for which he was paid $1 million per episode as a successful, professional actor and comedian. He was found floating unresponsive in a hot tub in his Los Angeles home. Dead at age 54 he was a relatively young man who had the world by the tail. *The New York Times* reported that he was "rich, famous, and handsome." At the top of his game, he was living the so-called "good life." He had the status of a star, possessions, tons of money, fame, and fortune ... all the stuff the world tells me I must have to be happy and content. But, it wasn't enough. It never is. Perry spent more than half his lifetime (25 years) in and out of treatment and rehab centers— fifteen to be exact— trying to get on top of a nagging drug and alcohol problem that

---

[49] Randy Newman, Searching Again in a Post-Modern World, *The Washington Institute For Faith, Vocation and Culture,* Accessed December 10, 2024, retrieved from https://washingtoninst.org/searching-again-in-a-post-postmodern-world/

would not go away. He died from the "acute effects" of anti-depression drugs and opium.[50] I suspect that a life lived without purpose or meaning played a major role in his demise, not a "biomedical condition" or a "genetic predisposition." Living apart from God and looking in all the wrong places for personal satisfaction and fulfillment fed his addiction. He failed repeatedly, finding no relief from the emotional pain and inner suffering which often accompany those who live without plan or purpose.[51] The emptiness runs deep. The void is real. Only God can satisfy the deepest longing of a man or woman's heart. Nothing else. The French mathematician and philosopher, Blaise Pascal (1623-1662), was right on target. He said,

> *What else does this craving, and this helplessness, proclaim but that there was once in man a true happiness, of which all that now remains is the empty print and trace? This he tries in vain to fill with everything around him, seeking in things that are not there the help he cannot find in those that are, though none can help, since this infinite abyss can be filled only with an infinite and immutable object; in other words by God himself.*[52]

Who am I? Why am I here? Where am I going? Is that all there is? Questions that speak directly to the issue of the emptiness of humanity and the very reasons why we take up space on this old earth. There must be more than a six-foot hole in the ground awaiting us when we close our eyes for the last time. I am happy to tell you that there is. More than a hundred years ago, Christians sang,

---

[50] Ales Traub and Matt Stevens, Matthew Perry, star of 'Friends,' Is Dead at 54, *The New York Times*, October 9, 2023, retrieved from https://www.nytimes.com/2023/10/29/arts/television/matthew-perry-dead.html.

[51] Dr. David McNabb, president and CEO Adult and Teen Challenge Mid-South, Chattanooga, TN

[52] Blaise Pascal, *Pensées* (New York; Penguin Books, 1966), 75.

... This world is not my home
I'm just a-passing through
My treasures are laid up
Somewhere beyond the blue

... The angels beckon me
From heaven's open door
And I can't feel at home
In this world anymore

... Oh Lord, you know
I have no friend like you
If heaven's not my home
Then Lord, what will I do?

... The angels beckon me
From heaven's open door
And I can't feel at home
In this world anymore[53]

Maybe we should sing it again— a philosophy and focus for the whole of life right up to the final few days. Take life seriously. You only get one shot. One life. No more. Do it right the first time. There are no second chances, only a few limited opportunities while breath remains in our body to correct what is wrong and make daily life work. So, spend your days doing something of genuine value.

Reflect the love of God in Christ with those you rub shoulders with every day, everywhere. Invest heavily in the Kingdom of God and in the lives of people. That's what God wants from you (and me). He wants or needs nothing else ... except your heart. Get the heart, and you get everything else of the man thrown in.

Dick Staub, an award-winning broadcaster and writer, interviewed theologian and teacher R.C. Sproul about his conversion to Christ. I had the privilege of sitting in one of his

---

[53] Anonymous, This world is not my home (1919), Public Domain, retrieved from https://library.timelesstruths.org/music/This_World_Is_Not_My_Home/.

classes in seminary. He was an extraordinary communicator. Sproul indicated that he attended a church-related college on a football scholarship and admitted he had little to no interest in Christ. One night, he and his friend were headed out from campus for a night at the bars. Along the way, he was detoured and ended up talking to the captain on his football team for three hours. He was a strong Christian. During the interview Sproul said of that night,

> *This was the first person I ever met in my life that talked about Christ as a reality. I'd never heard anything like it. I was just absorbed, sat there for two or three hours. He didn't give a traditional evangelism talk to me; he just kept talking to me about the wisdom of the word of God. He quoted Ecclesiastes 11:3: "Whether a tree falls to the south or to the north, in the place where it falls, there will it lie." I just feel certain I'm the only person in church history that was converted by that verse. God just took that verse and struck my soul with it. I saw myself as a log that was rotting in the woods. And I was going nowhere.*
>
> *When I left that guy's table, I went up to my room. And in my room by myself, in the dark, I got on my knees and cried out to God to forgive me.*[54]

Sproul is gone now. He left this world and entered glory, having accomplished what God had sent him here to do. He lived a remarkable, productive life, all because one man took the time to speak truth into a life going nowhere, rotting and wasting away. There is so much more to life than Sproul once realized.

"God has created me to do Him some definite service" for which I am responsible to get the thing done. "He has committed some work to me which He has not committed to another. I have my

---

[54] The Dick Staub Interview: R. C. Sproul's Testimony, *ChristianityToday.com (12-30-02)*, retrieved from
https://www.preachingtoday.com/illustrations/2003/january/14162.html.

mission ... He had not created me for naught ... I shall do His work,"[55] so said Cardinal John Newman (1801-1890. I have that statement pasted in the front of my Bible since my early seminary days, over 50 years ago. God has intentionally brought me into this world. I am here for a reason. I have my place and a part to play of divine significance. I am important and necessary for God's purposes right up to my final breath. So are you.

In his book, *The Call: Finding and Fulfilling the Central Purpose of Your Life*, Os Guinness reminded us:

> *We are not our own; we have been bought with a price. We have no rights, only responsibilities. Following Christ is not our initiative, merely our response, in obedience ... Once we have been called, we literally 'have no choice.'*[56]

We live as God directs. You'll be better off for having done so.

The very first thing God did after forming man from the dust of the earth was to give him a purpose for living (Genesis 1:26-28). Adam had no choice in the matter. God was clear about what He required. There were no negotiations. No questions. No bargaining for better wages and benefits; just a straightforward, holy job description that gave all of mankind a specific focus, a special task to accomplish, a place, a position in this world, an important role to play this side of heaven, and a responsibility to live a life of consequence. God's expectations were clear as man was made accountable for the life God had given to him. Nothing has changed.

From the beginning, God expected Adam and Eve to use the time and skills they had been given wisely. He demands the same of me and you. He insists that I employ the gifts and talents He has built into my life to make the world I live in a better place and glorify His name in the process. He has placed me here to reflect His image

---

[55] Cardinal John Newman (1801-1890), 19th Century.
[56] Os Guinness, *The Call*, (Nashville, TN: Thomas Nelson, 2003), 167.

and character to a world that desperately needs to see Him and know Him personally and intimately, to bring the love and mercy of God to my neighbor, a cup of cold water when he/she is thirsty, an encouraging word to the dejected and the downcast who live on my street. We are called to be the hands and feet of Jesus in a world that needs help. God ordered it, demanded it, required it. And when we do it, our eyes are set toward eternity and our efforts have eternal value.

He has sent us out into our little corner of the earth, anointed and equipped by Him to bring *"Good News"* to the heart and soul of a wayward humanity. We are here, like Jesus, to speak and live out the grace and forgiveness of God, and in the name of Jesus set at liberty those held captive by the consequences of their own moral failures, poor choices, and destructive behavior. God has empowered me and you to apply the ointment of redemption to the eyes of the blind who have lost their way and see no way out of their predicament. He has called us to attend to the physical, spiritual, and emotional wounds of those discouraged and despondent. He has given to us the ability to help the fallen, the broken, and the destitute, and pour into their lives the *"balm of Gilead"* (Jesus) to soothe and heal the wounds that come with life in a fallen world (see Luke 4:18-19). We are divinely commissioned to engage the kingdom of darkness with the truth of God's Word and take the fight in the battle for the souls of men and women to the very gates of hell, to our generation and culture, and do so with a spiritual backbone, grit, and guts. We must never back down, but *"stand firm against the schemes of the devil"* (Ephesians 6:11).

When you do, you finally get down to God's business and live focused on God's design for daily living. Do you want something to do with your life? Well, here is a divine purpose for getting up in the morning— step out the door with eternity in view, and set about to fulfill your heavenly tasks as "a butcher, a baker, or a candlestick maker." Be Jesus in the world in which you live. Be a good husband, a good wife, a good neighbor, a dependable employee and employer, a man or woman of integrity, a man of faith with the heart of the Lion of Judah, loving God and people. '

Rick Warren identifies three questions every man or woman asks in one form or another, at some point in their lives:

1. The Question of Existence: Why am I alive?
2. The Question of Significance: Does my life matter?
3. The Question of Purpose: What on earth am I here for?[57]

Here is a summation of God's requirements and His purpose for our day-to-day lives straight from the Bible, God's Word to His people wanting to know how to live. It's really quite simple. *"And what does the Lord require of you? To act justly and to love mercy and to walk humbly with your God"* (Micah 6:8, NIV). That covers a lot of ground. A divine approach to daily living, a worldview that is *"good"* at any age.

I recently heard somebody say, "If there is a pulse, there is a purpose." Something to remember as you approach the end of your days.

Neither you nor I are here by accident. I am on a divine assignment (Jeremiah 29:11), and so are you, placed here by the will of God to fulfill His specific purposes for our individual lives (Ephesians 1:11). Ray Ortlund, author and president of Renewal Ministries and an Emeritus Council member of The Gospel Coalition, reminds us that

---

[57] Rick Warren, What on earth am I here for? *Lifeway*, January 1, 2014, retrieved from https://www.lifeway.com/en/articles/purpose-driven-rick-warren-what-on-earth-am-i-here-for.

Your life, my life, is a story of divine prophetic intention. An ancient and glorious purpose is playing out through us today. Our hearts sense it. The Bible confirms it.[58]

Think bigger. Raise your faith. Be confident of what God can and wants to do in this world through you. Devote your final years to completing God's assignment. Do not let up. Not now. Even my old age may be a "steppingstone" to fulfilling the purpose and plan of God for my life. Be mindful and thoughtful of the choices you make, no matter how much or how little time you have left. There is more coming. This is not the end.

The final words of Saint Teresa of Avila (1515-1545), a Carmelite nun, are revealing. She whispered, "My Lord, it is time to move on. Well then, may Your will be done. O my Lord … the hour that I have longed for has come. It is time for us to meet one another."[59] One day we will all be saying that. Teresa had found her place in the world. She did the job she was called to do by God. She ran the race, stayed the course, and crossed the finish line, knowing there was more, much more to come.

For now, there is no question of God's influence and involvement in my life … right to the very end. He is directing my paths, ordering my steps, and preparing me for what lies ahead. And it is not the cemetery. My final destination is not the funeral parlor. There is yet more. Live in that expectation. I never thought I would ever say this, but Howard Stern was right. To believe and live like the morgue is our final resting place is "hard" and terribly depressing, to say the least.

---

[58] Ray Ortlund, Your life is prophetic, The Gospel Coalition, September 22, 2023, retrieved from https://www.thegospelcoalition.org/blogs/ray-ortlund/your-life-is-prophetic/.

[59] Mary Kris I. Figueroa, The last words of 40 saints before death, *The Best Catholic*, November 2, 2016, retrieved from https://www.thebestcatholic.com/2016/11/02/last-words-40-saints-death/.

In his classic, *The Making of a Man of God,* Alan Redpath, suggested that there are three things every man and woman needs "to exist and to survive: vision, passion, (and) action!" He then defined those terms.

- A vision of what can be.
- A passion for the things of God.
- A plan to fulfill God's purposes.[60]

Better to look forward, not back. Stay focused on the goal. *"Keep seeking the things above ... set your mind on the things above, not on the things that are on earth"* (Colossians 3:1-2), for your own well-being and the glory of God. And continue to do so until the day God shouts, "Enough!" and calls you and me to come on Home. The hymnwriter reminds us:

While we walk the pilgrim pathway
Clouds will overspread the sky;
But when trav'ling days are over
Not a shadow, not a sigh.

When we all get to heaven,
what a day of rejoicing that will be!
When we all see Jesus,
we'll sing and shout the victory!"[61]

That is where my eyes will rest. That is where my passion lives, until my heart stops beating.

Lutheran pastor, Dietrich Bonhoeffer (1906-1945), a man who saw death as "the last station on the road to freedom"[62] was found guilty of treason and executed by Nazi Germany just before the end

---

[60] Alan Redpath, *The Making of a Man of God: Studies in the Life of David*, (London: Pickering &Inglis LTD, 1963, 129-130.

[61] E.E. Hewitt, *When We All Get to Heaven*,1898, Public Domain, retrieved from https://hymnary.org/text/sing_the_wondrous_love_of_jesus_sing_his.

[62] Eric Metaxas, *Bonhoeffer, Pastor, Martyr, Prophet, Spy: A Righteous Gentile vs. the Third Reich*, (Nashville, TN: Thomas Nelson, 2010), 351.

CHAPTER 6: SET YOUR EYES TOWARD HEAVEN. THERE IS MORE TO COME.

of World War II. He passionately believed that "life only really begins when it ends here on earth, that all that is here is only prologue before the curtain goes up ... (death) is the gateway to our homeland, the tabernacle of joy, the everlasting kingdom of peace."[63]

Dr. H. Fischer-Hullstrung was with Bonhoeffer during his final minutes. He gave this account:

> *Pastor Bonhoeffer was kneeling on the floor praying fervently to his God. I was most deeply moved by the way this lovable man prayed, so devout and so certain that God heard his prayer ... (he) climbed the steps to the gallows, brave and composed ... (he died) "a few seconds (later). In the almost 50 years that I worked as a doctor, I have hardly ever seen a man die so entirely submissive to the will of God.*[64]

Oh, may that be me! An extraordinary man who lived an extraordinary life and served an extraordinary God. His task was done. His reward was waiting. And he knew it.

Faithfulness and servanthood over the long haul characterized Bonhoeffer's short life right up to the moment he marched up to the gallows, breathed his last, and entered glory. It is the stuff of kingdom living from the cradle to the grave.

Chuck Colson had a small sign on his desk. It simply read, "Faithfulness, not success."[65] The focus of daily Christian living and reason enough to finish strong with eternity in view. Heaven is just ahead! *"And I can't feel at home, in this world anymore ... "*

---

[63] Ibid.
[64] Ibid, 352.
[65] John Stonestreet and Dr. Glenn Sunshine, The Long, Faithful Obedience of William Wilberforce, *Breakpoint Daily Colson Center,* March 14, 2025, retrieved from https://mail.google.com/mail/u/0/

> *"You'll be home soon, too. You may not have noticed it, but you are closer to home than ever before. Each moment is a step taken. Each breath is a page turned. Each day is a mile marked, a mountain climbed. You are closer to home than you've ever been.*
>
> *Before you know it, your appointed arrival time will come; you'll descend the ramp and enter the City. You'll see faces that are waiting for you. You'll hear your name spoken by those who love you. And, maybe, just maybe— in the back, behind the crowds—the One who would rather die than live without you will remove his pierced hands from his heavenly robe and...applaud."*[66]
>
> –Max Lucado, *The Applause of Heaven*

CHAPTER 7

The Grace Of God. I Need Every Bit I Can Get!

Grace works best amidst our greatest failures, foolishness, and moral regrets when the heart breaks with disappointment over the knowledge that we've personally and royally screwed up. And I've done my fair share of reckless behavior, stupid decisions, selfish attitudes, and rebellious actions.

George Müller (1805-1898) is best known for his rescue of orphans from the streets of Bristol, England. He founded a ministry birthed from a heart of faith. He showed us how to live in full

---

[66] Max Lucado, *The Applause of Heaven,* (Nashville, Tennessee: Thomas Nelson, 1999), 183.

dependance and reliance upon God to meet the greatest needs of desperate children by providing a roof over their heads, clothes on their backs, food on the table, and an education to prepare them for life as an adult. Few know that prior to his walk with God, Müller spent more than a year in prison during his youth. He was a thief and a prolific liar. He admitted, "I was guilty of gross immorality … I did not care in the least about God … I had no sorrow of heart on account of offending God."[67] But then "God began a work of grace" in Müller, and his life dramatically changed for the better.[68] The life of a sinful, self-absorbed, wretched man was redeemed from the pit of hell. His sins were forgiven and mercy and divine power made him a new man, an instrument of love to the glory of God. Grace did its work. It always does.

I admit that I, too, am a rebel by choice who forever stands in need of God's continual grace and forgiveness. I have not made the divine grade, having often come up short of being the man God wants me to be. I readily accept my need for grace, and I might add, I need a lot of it. You cannot fully grasp the depth of God's grace until you understand the deep trouble we are in. A.W. Tozer defined grace as the following:

> *The good pleasure of God that inclines Him to bestow benefits upon the undeserving (that's definitely me). It is a self-existent principle inherent in the divine nature … to pity the wretched, spare the guilty, welcome the outcast, and bring into favor those who were before under just disapprobation (divine displeasure and disapproval) … Grace takes its rise far back in the heart of God, in the awful and incomprehensible abyss of His*

---

[67] *George* Muller, *The Autobiography of George Muller,* (OK Publishing, Kindle Edition, 2020), 24-26.
[68] Ibid, 26

holy being; but the channel through which it flows out to men is Jesus Christ, crucified and risen.[69]

Obviously, grace is more than "unmerited favor."

Over the years, I have become increasingly aware of my own shortcomings and moral flaws and have repeatedly wept before God over each one. I see the fool I once was, and in many respects, continue to be. It is not a pretty picture by any stretch of the imagination. The hymn writer had me in mind when he wrote these chilling words— "prone to wander, Lord, I feel it. Prone to leave the God I love."[70] A clear indictment of my failures.

I am reminded of one of William Shakespeare's most intriguing characters, Lady Macbeth, who heard a prophecy that her husband would become king and convinced him to assassinate the reigning monarch. When the bloody deed was done, Macbeth was conscience-stricken. His wife rebuked him, scolded him for the guilt he felt for the murder he had committed, and then she helped him cover up the crime. Her husband was crowned king. But that was not the end.

Lady Macbeth's initial resolve turned to remorse. She grew mentally unstable, and

couldn't stop washing her hands. "Will these hands ne'er be clean?" she asked. In the end, the burden of her guilt (see Psalm 32 and 51) drove Lady Macbeth to take her own life to end her pain.

"Will these hands ne'er be clean?" has been asked in one form or another by many a man or woman. The question is a plea for relief from the weight of self-serving, destructive decisions and actions that have violated the code of decency expected of all human beings. It is a painful declaration, a confession of sorts, a clear reminder that life should have been lived on a higher plane but wasn't. It is an admission that I have repeatedly and downright miserably failed

---

[69] A.W. Tozer, *The Knowledge of the Holy,* (Kindle Edition, 2019), 50.
[70] Robert Robinson, *Come, Thou Fount of Every Blessing*, 1758, Public Domain.

myself and others, but more importantly, I have failed God, who I know cannot be pleased with my choices. In short, I have not done well either historically or recently, all of which has left me with a sense of great, personal remorse and regret. More to the point, I have a thorough disgust for my lack of inner integrity, and I am left forever trying to "wash my hands" of the guilt, like Lady Macbeth. A universal, moral law truthfully and accurately reflects back to my soul's eye with brutal honesty, a glimpse at my current condition and what I really am: stained, tainted, damaged, even corrupt. I am not very "clean." My hands are "dirty." Thank God for the cross of Christ, where *"the grace of God ... can save every man, has now become known, (teaching) us to have no more to do with godlessness or the desires of this world but to live, here and now, responsible, honorable and God-fearing lives."* (Titus 2:11-12, PHILLIPS).

One person admitted to me about his Christian life, "Most of the time I fail more often than I succeed!" I don't know about you, but I can relate.

I am pulling no punches here (and neither should you). I have walked too close to the precipice of personal ruin and destruction to treat my weaknesses and failings lightly. I have a long rap sheet, as you might have guessed. The guilt of nearly tossing away the life God has given me is a heavy burden on my soul. I know it and shudder to think of the deep pain I might have caused and the blessings I might have missed had I persisted down a path of willful, determined disobedience to the laws of God, doing what I knew I should not do, defiantly and deliberately. And, I might add, there are always consequences. A man or woman can die a thousand deaths before his/her foot ever hits the grave. Not to worry, the Devil will gladly see that you get what you have earned: no mercy.

I am certain that the wages of sin is death. I've seen it, felt it, and lived it. But the story doesn't stop there.

God stepped in ... and divine grace flowed down in life-giving droplets of blood from the cross and into my life. Once I was *"dead in trespasses and sins."* Now I am *"made alive"* by the love and grace of God (see Ephesians 2:1-5). Subsequently, I have grown exponentially with each passing day in awareness and appreciation for God's saving grace than at any time in my nearly eighty years. I wholeheartedly concur with C.H. Spurgeon who said, "While others are congratulating themselves, I have to sit humbly at the foot of the cross and marvel that I'm saved at all."[71] Max Lucado wrote in his book, *Wild Grace*, "To get to the good stuff—grace—we first have to accept that we're neck-deep in the bad stuff called sin."[72] That is my story, and before you get too puffed up, I dare say that is part of yours, too. Faith is me looking to God and God alone. The grace of God is how God turns to me and meets me in my fallenness and deals with the "junk" in my life.[73] At my age, I've got a lot of junk piled up. The "garbage" heap is quite sizable.

Paul wrote to the church at Rome, *"Where sin increased, grace abounded all the more"* (Romans 5:20). I have a lot of sin, but I've been given a lot of grace. It's a good thing and a great lesson worth learning, living, and remembering as the end of your days and mine closes in. I want to finish strong, boasting only *"in the cross of our Lord Jesus Christ, through which the world has been crucified to me, and I to the world"* (Galatians 6:14) or as Phillips translates the phrase, *"the world is a dead thing to me, and I am a dead man to the world."* Grace is the work of God that grants me freely (don't miss that) without strings attached, His abundant love, a transformed life, a clear mind, a soft heart, and a joy unspeakable and undeserved. More than a 100 years ago, the hymn writer, Julia Johnston, captured the essence of God's love. She called it

---

[71] C.H. Spurgeon, Quote, Tulip Gospel Outreach, no date, retrieved from https://www.tulipgospeloutreach.org/quote/post/spurgeon-foot-of-the-cross.
[72] Max Lucado, *Wild Grace*, (Nashville, Tennessee: Thomas Nelson, 2012), 46.
[73] Ibid, 9.

"Marvelous grace, grace that exceeds (my) sin and (my) guilt ... to pardon and cleanse within ..."[74]

When Nehemiah finished rebuilding the walls of Jerusalem, he gathered the people together and had Ezra read the Scriptures to the crowd that had gathered (Nehemiah 8:13-9:1-38). He opened the scroll and gave them a history lesson, reviewing their journey (their miserable track-record) through the years. In short, they were stubborn, rebellious, and arrogant, thinking they knew more and better than God, and proved themselves repeatedly to be unfaithful and ungrateful toward God, who had treated them well, provided for their every need, and guided them through the desert. In the end, they thumbed their noses in the face of Almighty God. It all sounds like a running commentary of my own life and probably yours.

However" and "Nevertheless" (Nehemiah 9:30-31) are the two words that catch my attention and bring the love of God forward into my life thousands of years later. They define the grace and mercy of God in my story. *"Nevertheless, in Thy great compassion Thou didst not make an end of them (me) or forsake them (me)"* (v. 31), no matter what the Israelites had done, how they had disappointed God and themselves, or how many times they tried to shake free of God's word and will. God simply wouldn't let them go. *"(He) bore ... and admonished them"* (v. 30 – the action is continual). His longsuffering (love stretched out over the long haul) has never and will never end. God stayed with them every step of the way (Nehemiah 9:16-17, 28-29), as He has done in your life and mine.

That's divine, forever-love, non-stop, unending compassion, and abundant mercy. There is no place God won't go to grab you, if necessary, by the scruff of your neck and drag you and me "kicking

---

[74] `Julia H. Johnson, Grace Greater Then Our Sin, Public Domain, 1910, retrieved from
https://hymnary.org/text/marvelous_grace_of_our_loving_lord

and screaming" (C.S. Lewis) into His kingdom, rescuing us *"from the kingdom of darkness and transferred us into the Kingdom of his dear Son, who purchased our freedom (redemption) and forgave our sins* (Colossians 1:13-14, NLT). The results are clear: life not death, light not darkness, liberty not bondage, and a future not hopelessness. Get this straight. There is no place so dirty or so dark that God can't find you.

I confess that through the years, God has *"dealt faithfully (with me), but (I) have acted wickedly"* (v. 33). And that about sums it up. It's unbelievable. He will not let you or me go, no matter how bad yesterday looks or how tough or scary today may seem. Your future and mine are secure in the love of Christ. He will never abandon you, never write you off, never dismiss you as unimportant, worthless, or insignificant. Others may, but God does not. Remarkable, extraordinary, uncommon, inexhaustible, divine grace: I need a lot of that.

In the heat of the day in a Burmese village, Adoniram Judson (1788-1850) preached under the open sky, his voice weakened by years of suffering—imprisoned in the worst of conditions, starvation, loneliness, beatings, such hopelessness, and the death of his wife and several children.[75] He was an older man now, but his heart still burned with the message of the Gospel and eternity. Faith in God was the "ruling principle" in Judson's later life despite the unimaginable level of suffering he experienced on the mission field for the sake of the Gospel and the souls of men and women. He endured much for the cause of Christ but never lost his *"first love"* (Revelation 2:4) for the Son of God, Jesus.

Among the crowd that day, sat an older man. He had stone-cold eyes and scars on his face to match. No one dared speak to him.

---

[75] J.D. Greear, The conversion of Adoniram Judson, *J.D. Ministries,* October 8, 2012, retrieved from
https://jdgreear.com/the-conversion-of-adoniram-judson/

He was, after all, the royal executioner in the Kingdom of Ava (upper Burma), tasked with beheading prisoners and the torturing of countless others. He was a brutal, intimidating man whose heart had grown terribly calloused by the things he had done. He was assigned to the very prison where Judson was jailed and watched him slowly rot away.

The former executioner sat cross-legged in the dirt, unmoved and unemotional, while Judson spoke of the love of God and the Christ who uttered from the cross, *"Father, forgive them; for they know not what they do."* The troubled man began to tremble. His heart was pierced by the words of the Lamb of God. Tears formed in his eyes. When the message ended, he slowly approached Judson and dropped to his knees in repentance, a broken man. "I heard this man cry that same thing," he whispered, "when I beat him in (the prison at) Ava. He prayed for me … while I tortured him."[76] He wept aloud, and the grace and mercy of God reached a cruel, heartless man, penetrated his hardened soul, brought him to his knees, and upended his entire life.

On his deathbed, Judson uttered the following words:

> *I suppose they think me an old man, and imagine it is nothing for one like me to resign a life so full of trials. But I am not old—at least in that sense; you know I am not. Oh, no man ever left the world with more inviting prospects, with brighter hopes, or warmer feelings.*[77]

The work of Adoniram Judson left 7,000 believers behind in Burma. He lived, spoke, and ministered the grace of God, which changed the lives of so many. That's how I want to go out, riding the crest of God's grace and the privileges associated with serving the King in the place of His choosing, no longer living for myself, *"but*

---

[76] The story retrieved from Facebook, April 26, 2026, The Daily Spurgeon Group, The conversion of the executioner.
[77] *Op.cite*, Judson.

for Him who died and rose again on my behalf" (2Corinthians 5:14-15). The grace of God: I need every bit I can get.

Soren Kierkegaard (1813-1855), Danish theologian and philosopher, believed that there existed a great divide between God and man that could only be bridged by Jesus Christ. During the Age of Enlightenment, Kierkegaard challenged the church of his day that emphasized human potential and reason over a lost humanity needing redemption and faith in the Son of God. He prayed,

> *Father in Heaven! Hold not our sins up against us but hold us up against our sins so that the thought of You when it wakens in our soul, and each time it wakens, should not remind us of what we have committed but of what You did forgive, not of how we went astray, but of how You did save us!*[78]

"For by grace you have been saved through faith and that not of yourselves (It's never been about you or me anyway), *it is the gift of God... that no man should boast"* (Ephesians 2:8-9). The verse could be translated, *"By grace you are (and will continue to be) having been saved."* Clearly, salvation is God's work from start to finish, and, I might add, He does not do things half-hearted, nor leave His work undone, or ask flesh and blood to do what it will never do apart from God Himself—bring life to a spiritually dead corpse, or, in today's language, to the *"walking dead." "When we were dead in our transgressions,"* Paul wrote, "(God and only God) made us (me) alive with Christ (Ephesians 2:5). Salvation is sure and not attached to the merits (whatever they be) of any man or woman. Sola gratis (grace and grace alone) was at the heart of the mid-16th century Reformation, which swept through Europe. Nothing has changed. The truth remains. Salvation was, is, and

---

[78] Robert Foster and James Bryan Smith, *Devotional Classics: Selected Readings for Individuals and Groups*, (New York, NY: HarperCollins, 1993), 107.

forever will be God-ordained, *"according to the kind intention of His will, to the praise of the glory of His grace, which He freely (don't miss that) bestowed (poured out) on us ..."* (Ephesians 1:5). The grace of God will not permit the God of our salvation to do otherwise. It was His good pleasure from the start, *"before the foundation of the world"* (Ephesians 1:4).

The three most important words ever uttered by Jesus were spoken while He hung crucified on a cross. Just three words changed the world and changed my life— *"It is finished"* (John 19:30). In that moment, divine grace was poured out upon all humanity. A holy price was paid. My redemption was purchased. My debt was settled. My forgiveness was secured. My record was expunged ... forever. We dare not forget the grace of God, which encompasses the whole of biblical revelation and impacts my life and yours in extraordinary ways. It is one thing to read about grace. It is quite another matter to experience it for oneself.

Some years ago, I told the following story. I attended the NAIA National Men's Basketball Tournament. My son was playing. He was the co-captain and the starting point guard that year, leading the men's college team to their one and only trip to the "Big Dance." It had never happened before, and it hasn't happened since. He had a marvelous basketball career—a solid defender, smart with the ball, a consistent, unselfish player, and a threat from the outside, shooting over 50 percent from the 3-point line.

The opening tournament game, however, ended with a loss. His career was over. It was his final game. He would not play another. He knew it. His father knew it. It was finished. I walked into the locker room following the game to find my son. He had not yet arrived. He had lingered a bit longer out on the court. I waited. Finally, the door opened and in he walked. Our eyes met, and we came together in the middle of that locker room and embraced. There was silence. Nothing needed to be said. Nothing should have been said. It was a special moment between father and son. I will never forget it.

In those few moments, my mind flashed back over the years. I recalled those times when he was a little boy in the driveway, teaching him how to shoot a basketball. I thought of his days in the local, community basketball leagues when as an eight year old he would emerge from a group of ten players and race down the court with the ball. I remembered him leading his high school team to a state championship, averaging 28 points a game and being named the state tournament Most Valuable Player his senior year. I remember the tears rolling down my cheeks, as I stood in the stands applauding the achievements of my son. I thought of the previous four years and the game-winning shots, the joy of watching him play college ball with passion and an uncommon determination to win. But now, it was over.

In retrospect, it wasn't so much *what* I thought about while embracing my son at the end of his basketball career, but *what I didn't* think about which I found so remarkable. I never thought of those times he dribbled the ball off his foot. I never thought of that time he sprinted down the court only to make an errant pass to throw the ball away. I never once thought of those moments he missed a shot or got angry at an official for making a questionable call. I had not one thought of my son's past failures, not even for a second. In the end, I thought only of his successes, his victories, his achievements, his smile—those moments when he excelled and surpassed the ordinary and simply did well. And I thought ...

> *Lord, is this the way it is going to be with me and You, when I've come to the end of my life; when my years are finished, my days are complete, the whistle has blown, and the 'game' is over?*

I wondered...

> *When our eyes finally meet in Eternity and we stand face to face, will You, Father, lovingly embrace me and share with me those few special moments that only a Father and son can experience, remembering only my successes, only my triumphs, and giving no thought to my failures, my missteps, or my misguided decisions and actions?*[79]

The answer is found in the simple message of the Cross, in the promise of God, *"And their sins and their lawless deeds, I will remember no more"* (Hebrews 10:17, NASB). God refuses not to love me or you.

I didn't learn that in a seminary classroom. I learned it in an old, gym locker room, filled with the musty odor of sweaty uniforms, athletic tape, and wet towels.

"Grace and peace be multiplied to you in the knowledge of God and of Jesus our Lord" (2 Peter 1:2). Consequently, it is the only thing that truly matters … the mysterious, unexplained, outrageous grace of God and the peace it brings to my life and yours.

Isaac Watts understood the grace of God. He wrote these words in 1707, some 300 years ago:

> *When I survey the wondrous cross*
> *on which the Prince of glory died,*
> *my richest gain I count but loss,*
> *and pour contempt on all my pride.*
>
> *Were the whole realm of nature mine,*
> *that were a present far too small.*
> *Love so amazing, so divine,*
> *demands my soul, my life, my all.*[80]

---

[79] Sanford Zensen, *On the Wall with Sword and Trowel*, (Eugene, Oregon: WIPF and Stock, 2019), 54-56.
[80] Isaac Watts, *When I Survey the Wonderous Cross*, 1707, Public Domain.

Finish strong as you prepare to enter the gates of eternity. And if you listen carefully, you may hear the applause of heaven upon your arrival. It is the sound of divine grace. Go get yourself some.

> *"Even to your old age and gray hairs, I am he, I am he (or I will be the same, NASB) who will sustain you. I have made you and I will carry you; I will sustain you and I will rescue you."*
>
> –God (Isaiah 46:4, NIV)

CHAPTER 8

Feed On The Faithfulness Of God And A Good Slice Of Pizza

I've heard it said (not sure who said it), "Sometimes getting out of bed just ruins the whole day." That's no lie. I know firsthand There is a better way to view and approach daily living with all its ups and downs. Learn to lean on the faithfulness of God. In short, know that He has your back ... always, no matter what the circumstances. Nothing can change that. It's the truth. I can count on Him to be fully present in my life to support, provide, and protect my every move. You would think that after all these years I would have learned to relax and rest more fully in the person and power of God. I haven't. I've not always handled life well. For my part, trusting God has lacked consistency, often producing an anxious spirit, sleepless nights, and runaway thoughts that just keep right on running ... like the Energizer Bunny who never seems to quit. I can worry with the best of them.

Knowing God more deeply and intimately is the key to raising the level of trust in Him, helping us leave life with all its uncertainties for God to figure out. Christ said, *"Come to Me ...learn* (imperative) *of Me,"* hold fast to what you know of God, and the divine promise is, He *"will give rest to your soul"* (Mattthew 11:28-29). That is, "deliverance from every fear, the supply of every want, the fulfillment of every desire"[81] that fits within the context of God's will and word.

The Auburn Tigers Men's Basketball Team marched into the Final Four of the 2025 NCAA National Basketball Tournament. They beat Michigan State to advance. In the post-game interview, Johni Broome, the Tigers' star player, said, "All glory to God. When I came back out (of the locker room following an injury to a standing ovation), I hit that three-ball. I called on Him (God) again. You got to always call on Him. He's always going to deliver."[82] And therein is the faithfulness of God to always deliver. He loves. He hears. He acts. Count on it.

God alone can be trusted to be and act always in accordance with His character and nature, and no other way. It is His nature to keep His promises, to fulfill His covenant vows and stipulations, and to love and care for His creatures and creation. That never changes, because He never changes. There is a "divine constancy"[83] found in the heart of God. At the core of His being, He is God, and acts like God always, every time, be it in the desert with Moses or on a basketball court with Johni Broome. God said of Himself, *"I Am Who I Am, and What I Am, and I Will Be What I Will Be"* (Exodus

---

[81] Murray, Andrew. Abide in Christ, Large Print Edition, Burten Classics, Kindle Format, July 2021, 144.

[82] Kevin Mercer, Johni Broome 'called on Him' as he powers Auburn into Final Four: 'All glory to God,' *Sports Spectrum Magazine,* March 31, 2025, retrieved from https://sportsspectrum.com/sport/basketball/2025/03/31/johni-broome-auburn-final-four-all-glory-to-god/.

[83] Millard J. Erickson, *Christian Theology*, (Grand Rapids, Michigan: Baker Book House, 1985), 279.

3:14, AMPC). You will find Him to be enough. He cannot be other than Who He is. *"We know how much God loves us,"* wrote John,

> *"and we have put our trust in his (unchanging, eternal, unending, continuing) love. God is love (and that remains forever) ... So we will not be afraid on the day of judgment, but we can face him with confidence (because the nature of God never changes) ... Such love has no fear, because perfect love expels all fear"* (I John 4:16-18, NLT).

Since the day you were born to the day you die, God remains kindhearted, generous, merciful, longsuffering (love stretched out over the long haul), wise, always doing right, a gentle Father cradling His children, a good Shepherd protecting His flock, the King of all kings, ruling the universe forever, *"the Alpha and the Omega, says the Lord God, who is and who was and who is to come"* (Revelations 1:8), a Warrior with sword unsheathed to wage war and conquer the world, and ... *"eyes a flame of fire"* set and fixed toward ultimate and complete victory (Revelation 1:14, 19:12), and a name tattooed on Himself, *"which no one knows"* (Revelations 19:12). and so much more, more than my thoughts could possibly conceive, or conjure up. He is indescribable, unimaginable, incomprehensible. There can be no other. He alone is God. *"Hear O Israel, The Lord is our God. The Lord is one"* (Deuteronomy 6:4). God is unique, exclusive, the only One. *"LORD, there is no one like you! For you are great, and your name is full of power"* (Jeremiah 10:6, NLT). Feast of these truths.

A barren Hannah passionately *"poured out (her) soul before the Lord,"* seeking the only One she knew could help (1 Samuel 1:15). She prayed, *"There is no one holy like the Lord (Jehovah/Yahweh,* the Promise-Keeper, the One *"abounding in lovingkindness and truth")*.[84] *Jehovah* is God's personal name, and it appears approximately 5,500 times in the Old Testament.[85] But Hannah doesn't stop there. She gave us further insights into who God is and what He is like. She spoke with confidence and an uncommon boldness. *"Indeed, there is no one besides Thee, nor is there any rock like our God (Elohim, "the Creator of heaven and earth to whom all power belongs)"* (1 Samuel 2:2). He alone is God, *"able to make you* (Now, get this. Don't miss it) *stand in the presence of His glory blameless with great joy"* (Jude 1:24). And happy to do it! Can you imagine? Chew on that for a while.

With the city of Jerusalem in utter chaos, under siege, and with no means of escape from their enemies, Jeremiah stood in tears, surveying the inevitable fall of Jerusalem. The people would suffer certain defeat and disaster (586 B.C.) and be forcibly deported to Babylon. No one smiled. No one celebrated the move. The future looked grim. No one was singing, *"Don't Worry. Be Happy,"* on the march into slavery. There would be no joy in that parade. No balloons. No clowns. *"A broken heart crushes the spirit"* (Proverbs 15:13), so wrote Solomon, the wisest man who ever lived.

At his lowest point, emotionally distraught and spiritually whipped, Jeremiah reminded himself and the people of Judah of the truth about God, a truth that would carry them (and you and me) through the roughest days for some seventy years.

> **Lamentations 3:22–24, MSG** – *GOD's loyal love couldn't have run out, his merciful love couldn't have dried up. They're created new every morning. How great your faithfulness! I'm sticking with GOD (I say it over and over). He's all I've got left.*

God is enough. Believe it. Experience Him for yourself.

---

[84] Robert B. Girdlestone, *Synonyms of the Old Testament*, (Grand Rapids, Michigan: Wm. G. Eerdmans, 1897), 39.
[85] Ibid, 35.

Old age can be tough, often unpredictable, and utterly disruptive. It is easy to lose our smile in the daily chaos, the never-ending trips to the doctor's office, the stress of limited finances, and the death of family and longtime friends. Life is in constant flux, ever changing, and not necessarily for the better. I need stability and security, as my life begins its final countdown. I am reminded of a wonderful poem written by Thomas O. Chisholm (1923), which later became a great hymn of the church. Chisholm said that "there was no dramatic story behind (its) writing,"[86] just the typical ebb and flow of daily life. He found this to be true:

Great is Thy faithfulness, O God my Father
There is no shadow of turning with Thee
Thou changest not, Thy compassions, they fail not
As Thou hast been, Thou forever will be

Great is Thy faithfulness
Great is Thy faithfulness
Morning by morning new mercies I see
All I have needed Thy hand hath provided
Great is Thy faithfulness, Lord, unto me

At seventy years old,[87] Job looked out over the ten graves of his children. He had lost everything. I can't even imagine what was going through his mind. His wife wanted to know where God was when all hell broke loose in their lives. This was real life, and bad things do happen to good people. Job was hurting. His wife was bitter. She once may have thought she could trust God. But no more. Not now. Not after this tragedy. This was no laughing matter. *"Curse*

---

[86] Robert J. Morgan, *Then Sings My Soul*, (Nashville, Tennessee: Thomas Nelson, 2003), 285.
[87] Tony Chan, How old was Job when he suffered? *Bible Verse Commentary*, Reddit, retrieved from https://www.reddit.com/r/BibleVerseCommentary/comments/14f7cmr/how_old_was_job_when_he_suffered/#:-:text=%2D%20After%20this%20lived%20Job%20an,of%20the%20Bible%2C%20vol.

God and die," she screamed (Job 2:9). Job refused. He said, *"God gives and God takes away"* (see Job 1:21). Job decided to hang in there with God, though his hopes and dreams for himself and his family were buried six feet under the ground. In his despair, Job's friend, Bildad, tried to encourage him. *"He (God) will once again fill your mouth with laughter and your lips with shouts of joy"* (Job 8:21). Good news for an elderly gentleman, who needed to hear a comforting word. And, so do I.

When the clouds roll in and the storms are blowing hard, it is so easy to forget the goodness of God and His faithfulness through the years. I've taken God for granted. I've overlooked the fact that God has been there for me and you all along. Every morning when I open my eyes, God is present before my feet ever hit the floor. He has been good to me and you. *"Sing to the Lord a new song, for He has done marvelous* (extraordinary, surpassing, exceedingly great) *things"* (Psalm 98:1). Remember them. *"Bless (affectionately and gratefully speak well of) the Lord, O my soul, and forget not [one of] all His benefits"* (Psalm 103:2, AMPC). Recall the wonders of what God has done every day of your life—a great way to start each morning. It will put a smile on the face of any grumpy, old man or woman stepping out his/her front door to face whatever (good or bad) is coming their way. *"A cheerful heart,"* after all, *"is good medicine, but a broken spirit saps a person's strength."* (Proverbs 17:22, NLT).

Eric Metaxas was speaking at the Lee University chapel, where he told the story of his conversion to Christianity. He spoke of a dream where he was ice fishing and "Jesus Christ Son of God Our Savior" appeared to him as a living, gold, bronze-colored fish. It sounded a bit crazy. On the way out of the chapel service, a freshman student was heard to say sarcastically, "Yeah, maybe God will speak to *me* in a dream!" He got what he wished for, though he had dismissed and mocked Metaxas's story. Metaxas later connected with the student and discovered he had recently lost his mother to suicide. He had since been struggling with his faith, needing answers and healing, but not finding either. Later that night, following the chapel service, God showed up in the student's dream, which eventually led the young man to Christ. Metaxas wrote of the incident in his New York Times best-selling book, *Miracles*:

> *The idea that God would respond to someone's sarcastic crack about a dream by visiting him in a dream that night and changing his life in the same way is something that will encourage me for a long time.*[88]

Me, too. But isn't that just like God to show up in our lives and bring healing and wholeness to our wounded soul filled with doubts and fears, hang-ups, hurtful words, a critical spirit, and hateful behavior? It's a miracle. It's grace—the continual, persistent faithfulness and love of God at work in my life and yours. Isaiah recorded the words of God, *"For the mountains may move and the hills disappear, but even then my faithful love for you will remain ..."* (Isaiah 54:10, NLT), a promise and a song of restoration.

The psalmist wrote, *"Delight yourself in the Lord"* (Psalm 37:4). Good advice. The New American Standard Bible offers a powerful side note, an alternative translation that gets to the root of David's words. It reads, *"Feed on His (God's) faithfulness."* I love this profound reality and exhortation, important for every generation, old and young alike. God has repeatedly intervened in my life which has proven to be a consistent demonstration of His love and wisdom, encouraging my heart and lifting my spirit. Consequently, I am learning to count on God. Not there yet but moving forward. He took care of me yesterday. He is still doing that today, and He will do it again tomorrow. Suddenly, old age doesn't look so intimidating.

---

[88] Eric Metaxas, *Miracles*, (New York, New York: Penguin Books, 2014), 149.

There is no need to fret, panic, obsess, or wonder if God will come through for you. He will, right up to the very day He calls you home. Settle that issue. He has an ample supply of resources at His disposal for this life and the life to come. *"And my God shall supply (fill to the full) all your needs* (physical, emotional, mental, spiritual) *according to His riches in glory in Christ Jesus"* (Philippians 4:19). Now that's something to cheer about and rejoice over.

My wife and I recently ran into a friend, a wonderful Christian woman. We asked how her adult son, who had been hospitalized, was doing with his illness. She informed us that he was struggling physically with a debilitating, rare disease, for which the doctors had no answers. No cure. No medicine. No options that might help. He had battled this disease for more than ten years to no avail. He was tired and discouraged. No more fight left. He said so. His mother was heartbroken, understandably afraid and deeply concerned for the well-being of her son. She said, "I'm worried he might simply give up and quit." She sighed, "I guess I'm going to have to just trust the Lord with this whole thing." She was a woman desperately clinging to the hem of Christ's garment (see Luke 8:41-56) and hoping for the best. She resigned herself to God's plan (good move) and surrendered to God's sovereign will. Much like John the Baptist said, *"He must increase, but I must decrease. [He must grow more prominent; I must grow less] (John 3:30, AMPC).*

I immediately responded sarcastically to our friend, "So, it's come down to that, has it? —trusting God with your son's life? Who would have thought?" A rather callous remark. I was trying to lighten the moment. It didn't work. I could have and should have done differently. Maybe sharing a truth about God would have been better, not some arrogant, insensitive word. What I should have done was to feed her the *"bread of life"* to satisfy her anxious soul and encourage her troubled heart. I failed miserably.

I missed the opportunity to declare God's faithfulness, mercy, and power. I might better have said, "He is a miracle-working God.

He alone is the answer to your son's demise and your worry. Don't lose hope. Keep praying. God knows. Keep knocking. Keep seeking until God answers, and He will. *Oh, how He loves you and me."*[89] Now, that's better.

From Genesis to Revelation, the scriptures speak of God's faithfulness. You can't miss it. His promises are everywhere, and He delivers. *"The Lord your God is with you, he is mighty to save. He will take great delight in you, he will quiet you with his love, he will rejoice over you with singing"* (Zephaniah 3:17, NIV). How faithful and dependable is our God. David was on the run from his son, Absalom, who wanted his father dead and out of the way. One day, David started his morning with a song about God's faithfulness, particularly in a time of trouble. He penned the following words, *"O Lord, (You) are a shield for me, my glory, and the lifter of my head"* (Psalm 3:3, NIV). On another occasion, David spoke of God as *"My rock ... my salvation ... my fortress. I will not be shaken"* (Psalm 62:6, NIV). Those songs should be on the top ten list of every Christian. They are great songs, reminding me I can wholly depend on God. There is no question or doubt.

Paul reassured believers living under cultural pressure and persecution for their faith, *"Yet the Lord is faithful, and He will strengthen [you] and set you on a firm foundation and guard you from the evil [one]* (2 Thessalonians 3:3, AMPC). Learn to rest in Him. Charles Spurgeon said of those who truly know God and His nature and character,

> ...the Christian blesses (God) when he smites him: he believes him to be too wise to err and too good to be unkind; he trusts him where he cannot trace him, looks

---

[89] Kurt Kaiser, *Oh How He loves You and Me*. Word Music, LLC, 1975.

up to him in the darkest hour, and believes that all is well.[90]

That's good "food" for thought.

It is God who will strengthen your resolve to face the day and keep going. Elijah was wasting away in a cave, licking his emotional and spiritual wounds, running for his life (1 Kings 19:3), feeling sorry for himself, afraid and despairing over his situation, hopeless and alone. He wanted out. He wanted to die. But *"the word of the Lord came to him"* (1 Kings 19:9), and God sustained him and encouraged him with *"a bread cake baked on hot stones, and a jar of water"* (v.6). It was probably the first DoorDash ever recorded in history. God's messenger got Elijah to his feet, told him not to quit, and empowered him to keep going. God rides *"the heavens to (my) help"* (Deuteronomy 33:26) to change the course of my life, to bring a renewed passion and energy for living, and to restore my soul (I sure enough need some of that), and accomplish all God wants done in my life, regardless of my age. There is more to do even in my old age. Senior living, I've discovered, is more than shuffleboard, a round of golf, pickle ball, or lounging poolside doing he-man poses for the crowd.

God has been good to you and me all along the way, and He will continue to be, even in those trying moments when we doubt Him. He has stuck with you, even as He has stuck with me, when we've tried to run away from His presence. He took you back like the prodigal son, who had squandered his life; like Moses who ran from Egypt with his tail between his legs after murdering an Egyptian; and David the adulterer and murderer, whose lust and abuse of power nearly destroyed him; and Rahab the prostitute who was abused by men but used by God to carry out His plan; and a

---

[90] Charles H. Spurgeon, A Happy Christian, Metropolitan Tabernacle Pulpit Volume 13, 1867. retrieved from https://www.spurgeon.org/resource-library/sermons/a-happy-christian/#flipbook/.

vindictive Jonah who fled from the call of God upon his life to deliver a message of divine mercy to a people who didn't deserve it; and a young, arrogant, boastful Joseph, who exchanged his *"coat of many colors"* (Genesis 37:3) for prison clothes and later walked the halls of a palace; and then there was Gideon, *"a valiant warrior"* (Judges 6:12,) who cowered before the Midianites; and Paul, a Pharisee of Pharisees who formerly hated Jesus and fervently persecuted His followers. All "broken vessels" (see Psalm 31:12, 2 Corinthians 4:7), every one of them, that God faithfully and persistently loved, divinely reshaped, graciously renewed, and gave them life and the opportunity to become useful vessels in God's kingdom. It's been said, "God loves *cracked-pots."* That's all of us—the unlovable, the helpless, the destitute, the hopeless, the teenager, and the guy with one foot in the grave and slipping fast.

That's the message I should have delivered to that mother, who was trying desperately to hold on to her faith. *"God is not dead, and neither are you nor your son. God is good. God is faithful. Trust Him. Believe it. Live like it."* Not much more really needed to be said.

Here is a thought from Elisabeth Elliot: "If you believe in a God who controls the big things, you have to believe in a God who controls the little things." Sometimes I need to be rudely awakened and reassured of the sovereignty of God and His faithfulness. God does what He pleases, wherever He wants, whenever He wants, and with whomever He wants. His purpose is sure. His plans are secure. His goal is set. There is no *"shifting shadow"* (James 1:17) with God. Someone remind me to calculate a faithful God into daily living, especially when life is not going the way I want or when I am feeling old, useless, out of step, and out of place.

Frankly, God's ultimate purpose will not (nor can it) ever be denied, since the God of this universe, the One who has made Heaven *"His throne and the earth His footstool"* (Isaiah 66:1), declares the *"beginning and the end"* of every event in my life. He alone has the authority, power, and wisdom to bring all things (hurtful things, broken things, positive things) to their divinely appointed end in full compliance with His eternal, good plan. Even the tough stuff is used by God to secure His purpose for my life (see Romans 8:28), no matter what my age or in what circumstances I may find myself. In short, God has the last word in all matters, and that word is good, because He is good and faithful to do good in both the "big things" and the "little things." He cannot do otherwise.

Nahum, a minor prophet with a major message wrote, *"The Lord is good, a stronghold in the day of trouble, and He knows those who take refuge in Him"* (Nahum1:7). God has always been that, done that, and so much more throughout the course of my earthly existence. And He has no plans of stopping now, though things are drawing to a close and the curtain is quickly coming down on the story of my life.

Subsequently, I know where I must go to find *"refuge,"* to find shelter from despair, crippling self-pity, worry, doubts, and the insecurities that oftentimes accompany aging. I'm running to the *"fountain of life"* (Psalm 36:9) from which flows *"living water"* to drink deeply (John 7:37-38; see also Jeremiah 17:13) of the goodness and faithfulness of God. I know God is good, and I know He forever has my back. It is a lesson I've had to relearn … again … and again. It is God's goodness and His faithfulness that secures the "big things" and the "little things" in life. I know where I must head.

Following Pentecost, Peter, under the power of the Holy Spirit and in the name and authority of Jesus, healed a crippled beggar. The man, *"who had been lame from his mother's womb,"* was suddenly up on his feet, *"walking and leaping and praising God"* (Acts 3:9). Why not? He had gotten more from God than he ever expected; the faithfulness, power, and goodness of God. Regardless of age or circumstances, we all need the same.

Feed on that, and every now and then, go get yourself a good slice of pizza. You might be *"leaping and praising God,"* too.

"Come what may, let us trust and not be afraid. He will never lead us where His grace cannot keep us."[91]

CHAPTER 9

Celebrate Life No Matter How Bad It Gets

I love life, every bit of it, especially the successes, the triumphs, and the joy of achievement. But I've also come to see the value of setbacks, trials, loses, and failures, and I've had a good deal of that as well. It all counts, the ups and downs, the good days and the not so good days. Life hasn't always been easy. There have been disappointments, discouragements, disease; and death. Along the way, however, I've learned that even the painful experiences serve the interests of heaven and a God who knows what He's doing and knows how to bring His perfect will forward into my life. Romans 8:28 is for real. The passage doesn't say that all things are good. It says that "all things" (the good, the bad, and the ugly), the laughter, the tears, the victories and the defeats are used by God to weave His good and perfect purpose into our daily lives. The outcome of God's work is always good, always positive, always for our benefit and His glory. And I love it.

---

[91] Vance Havner, *Fourscore: Living Beyond the Promise,* (Old Tappen, New Jersey: F.H. Revell Company, 1982), 25.

This year Hailey Van Lith, star basketball player for Texas Christian University, averaging 17.4 points per game for the Horned Frogs, spoke openly and powerfully about the mental health struggles she has experienced throughout her collegiate career. She admitted that her life was lived in a dark place, in anguish and suffering internally and in silence. Nobody knew. Outwardly, she was successful, having won a bronze medal at the 2024 Paris Olympic Games, but her inner life was in complete disarray, disordered, even chaotic. She was miserable, emotionally spent, and despairing. She said, "I felt trapped, and you would never know because I was having a ton of success on the court, but internally and in life in general, I was ready to be done … I didn't even want to live." But God changed all that. Now she lives to "serve Jesus" and the interests of heaven. She explained,

> *I think that this is the year, and this is the moment that He wants people to know my story, and how He's taken me literally from the depths of wanting to die, to this moment of loving life. Even if basketball went away today, I truly would want to be here and love these people (teammates). So that's really my story with God and He's so powerful...Thank you God for carrying me to this moment. And thank you God in advance for the journey ahead of me*[92]

Life is worth living. Period. Win or lose. The providence of God, the presence, power and plan of God brings significance to my life, no matter what my age, for He has called me, raised me, equipped me, and guided me over the years to the time and place of His choosing to accomplish His will at every stage of my life. God

---

[92] Joshua Doering, Fueled by powerful testimony, TCU's Hailey Van Lith 'really standing on God's shoulders,' *Sports Spectrum Magazine*, Mar 25, 2025, retrieved from https://sportsspectrum.com/sport/basketball/2025/03/25/testimony-tcu-hailey-van-lith-standing-gods-shoulders/.

gives life value, even in the toughest of times. A great lesson for old guys and gals who may think and feel that there is nothing more to live for, nothing of any consequence left to do or say. But there is. The Scriptures lay out God's plan and purpose for how life is to be lived each day. Accordingly, we are to *"live…worthy of his call (and) to accomplish all the good things your faith prompts you to do"* (2 Thessalonians 1:11-12, NLT). In so doing, we *"honor"* God—the ultimate goal for Christ-centered living, which by the way, can't happen apart from the enabling power and grace of God. That holy objective for living out the Christian life has not been suspended or cancelled just because I have grown old. I am required to finish strong.

Eddie Jaku was severely beaten by the SS during the Nazi's rise to power in Germany. He was arrested and sent to a concentration camp along with thousands of other Jews. He lost everything—family, friends, possessions, social status, his freedom, and his future. He was alone, endured seven long years of unimaginable horror— starvation, executions, and the stench of ovens that cremated the bodies of Jews murdered in the gas chambers of the Third Reich. At the end of World War II, Eddie was liberated by the Allies, but feeling very much alone in the world. Everyone he loved and cherished, everything he knew was gone. He wrote in his memoirs following his release,

> *I had to decide what to do, to live or to find a tablet and die like my parents. But I made a promise to myself and to God to try to live the best existence I could, or else my parents' death and all the suffering would be for nothing. So I chose to live.*

It is a choice we all must make. Eddie Jaku called himself, *"The Happiest Man on Earth."*[93] Remarkable, considering the life

---

[93] Eddie Jaku, *The Happiest Man on Earth*, (New York, New York: HarperCollins, 2020), 136.

he lived and the darkness he walked through. In the prologue of his book, he summed up the lessons he learned about life, "... happiness is something we can choose. It is up to you." Today, he is 100 years old and smiling. We might consider the same approach as we grow old and face the days ahead with faith and a smile, even the hard days; They go together. So, choose life, whether you're moving through the mundane affairs of daily routines or shuffling along down the halls of the nursing home. The reality is that we are not finished, and God is not finished with either me or you. As long as there is breath in these old bones, God has something of great importance and significance for us in His kingdom and in this world. You may not see it that way, but that doesn't change the truth. I am still breathing, so I am ready and looking to serve Him in any capacity He chooses—love my family, love the church, love my neighbor as I love myself, and *"love the Lord (my) God with all (my) heart, with all (my) soul, and with all (my) mind* (Matthew 22:3-40). To do so, brings value to my life, even to an old, wrinkled-up, has-been, ready to be put out to pasture.

Just a smile or a word or two of encouragement for a broken, wounded person may seem small and trivial, but it's not. We bring the love of God into daily living. It *is* a big deal, especially in a world that knows so little of God's mercy and forgiveness. God has given me a place here and now that will impact eternity, as He has you. Irving Berlin said, "The song is ended but the melody lingers on.." And so does the impact of your life and mine long after we are gone.

After his incarceration in a German Nazi death camp where few survived, Victor Frankl (1905-1997) wrote, *Yes to Life: In Spite of Everything.* The title suggests that there is meaning in life, though the world has gone crazy with cruelty, destructive anger, the slaughter of innocence, hateful prejudices, racism, lawlessness, and self-serving and self-centered ideologies that drive it all forward, a description of the worst of our current culture and human nature. Examples abound—school shootings, the attempted murder of the President of the United States, the brutality of Hamas, the unrest on our streets, a media that cannot tell the truth, the disregard for the law, gender confusion, woke madness, the greed on Wall Street, and all the rest. What Frankl saw in the face of death and the horror of the gas chambers, the firing squads, the days and months of starvation, and the mass mistreatment and torture of people was nothing short of alarming. Horrific circumstances. Frankl himself on the brink of death, concluded that life was still a gift and still worth living and worth our greatest effort. A survivor of genocide offered a perspective of hope and endurance in the darkest of days. I am without excuse. I must not give up. I must stay productive, relevant, responsible, and say *Yes to life in spite of everything life brings us."* A principle that must be applied in our personal lives, especially when the daily grind gets hard and we are approaching the close of our days and feeling forgotten, abandoned, and of little worth. Apart from God, there is nothing more important than life.

The fact remains. I have value beyond my experiences, expertise, limitations, successes and failures. There is more to me than winning and losing. I have wisdom which comes from God above (James 1:5) and forged in the fires of tragedy and heartbreak. I have skills and God-given talents honed and chiseled by years of experience to make a real difference in my corner of the world. I have also been given a *"sensible"* mind (2 Timothy 1:7, NKJV), though some may say differently who know me. A *"renewed"* mind, however, comes from God, a mind that refuses to be conformed to this world, but transformed (Romans 12:1-3) and able to focus on the things above and below, an eternal perspective which connects earth to heaven and heaven to earth. Life is priceless, even if viewed from a wheel chair or a walker fully equipped with colorful streamers on the handle grips and bright yellow tennis balls attached to the front legs. I am ready to celebrate life, *"singing and making melody in (my) heart to the Lord"* (Ephesians 5:19). Party on old people…Finish strong.

> *"I question whether anyone has had a real encounter with the risen Lord Jesus at Calvary but that into his or her life has come a heavenly vision, a great determination, a holy resolve to the very best for Him—a glad, happy surrender of everything to the Master."*
>
> –Alan Redpath[94]

CONCLUSION

The Time of the End

At the conclusion of J.R.R. Tolkien's, *The Return of the King*, Gandalf, the White Wizard, stood with the two hobbits, Frodo and Sam. The end of a great journey had arrived. They had moved through each life event in a relentless effort to right all the wrongs that had followed them. At last, the infamous ring that had caused all the death, destruction, and darkness in the world had finally been eliminated. It was gone, tossed into the fires of Mt. Doom.

Gandalf and Frodo were about to get on the last ship bound for a greater land and new experiences beyond the distant horizon, wherever their imagination could take them. Their friends were in tears. This life was over. They embraced, knowing Frodo's departure

---

[94] Op.cite, Alan Redpath, 168.

was imminent. They begged him not to go. "You can't leave," they yelled. But leave, he must. "I will not say: do not weep;" said Gandalf, "for not all tears are an evil."

Frodo reached for his leather-covered journal, a record of his adventures, and turned to Sam, his closest friend. He handed him the book. "The last pages are for you, Sam." There were more tears ... understandably so. Everybody knew what this meant. Nothing would ever be the same. Friends would separate. Relationships would end, at least for a now. Yesterday passed, like it always does. And, all too quickly, if you ask me.

Frodo encouraged and challenged them. He seemed to be saying,

> *I've done what I was sent to do. My task complete. My purpose fulfilled. My journey is over. But not yours (or mine). There is more to come. Finish your story is my final word. Get on with your life, and write the ending, as only you can. It's yours to pen, your story to finish.*

I need to hear that. I suspect you do, too.

Gandalf looked at Frodo. "It is time," he said.[95] The time of the end had arrived, a time to leave yesterday behind and press forward to the celestial city, and there to *"drink from the spring of the water of life"* (Revelation 21:6) forevermore. I can assure you that when I have passed from this life to the next, I will be running, leaping, and shouting for joy, "Hallelujah!" all the way to the gates of heaven. The time of my final healing will most assuredly come for those who belong to the Father in Christ.

But for now, my life will stay the course mapped out for me by God, continuing the *"good fight,"* while I can still swing the *"sword of the Spirit, which is the word of God,"* and lift *"the shield*

---

[95] J.R.R. Tolkien (Novel), Screenplay by Fran Walsh, Philippa Boyens and Peter Jackson, *The Lord of the Rings: The Return of the King*, New Line Cinema, Release date in the United States, December 15, 2003.

of faith." (Ephesians 6:17-18). My objective is clear—to carry on, relentlessly pushing forward to *"where God is beckoning (me) onward—to Jesus. I'm off and running, and I'm not turning back"* (Philippians 3:14, MSG). In the interim, my job and yours will be to *"grow in the grace and knowledge of our Lord and Savior Jesus Christ. To him be glory both now and forever! Amen"* (2 Peter 3:18, NIV). Therefore, *"... run with endurance the race God has set before us ... keeping our eyes on Jesus"* (Hebrews 12:1). That is the end game—to finish and win the *"race"* (1 Corinthians 9:24), becoming the man or woman God desires us to be right up to the final moment. Persevere. Hang in there. Grow old with grace. After all, "Not all tears are an evil ..."

William R. Moody, the son of D.L. Moody, wrote a biography of his father, detailing the events and the work of God in the man's life. In the inside cover of that book, there is a short, revealing statement by D.L. regarding his life and subsequent death. He said,

> *Some day you will read in the papers that D.L. Moody, of East Northfield, is dead. Don't you believe a word of it! At that moment I shall be more alive than I am now, I shall have gone up higher, that is all; out of this old clay tenement into a house that is immortal—a body that death cannot touch; that sin cannot taint; a body fashioned like unto His (Jesus') glorious body.*
>
> *I was born of the flesh in 1837. I was born of the Spirit in 1856. That which is born of the flesh may die. That which is born of the Spirit will live forever.*[96]

And so it is for the person whose life has been touched by the grace, mercy, and goodness of God. I was born of flesh in 1946. I was born of the Spirit at a Billy Graham Crusade in Madison Square Garden,1957. God was there in that holy place, nudging me, moving

---

[96] William R. Moody, *The Life of Dwight L. Moody*, New York, New York: Fleming H. Reville Company, 1900), Inside book cover.

me, pressing me, urging me to leave my seat and make my way down from the upper balcony to the floor below to make a decision that would change the trajectory of my entire life. I couldn't say, "No," though I had no idea what my decision might mean, nor did I fully understand where God would eventually lead me, but I was going anyway. The Spirit of God mercifully drew me to Himself. He took me, *Just As I am*, an 11-year-old boy, wet behind the ears, despite my current failures and future sin. There would be plenty of personal shortcomings to come in the years ahead and sure evidence of human depravity.

> *Just as I am, without one plea,*
> *But that Thy blood was shed for me,*
> *And that Thou bid'st me come to Thee,*
> *O Lamb of God, I come! I come!*[97]

And I came, indeed! I remember it well. God saw my life past, present, and future and latched onto me regardless of the foolishness and rebellion yet to come. At no time did He ever let up or gave up on me. He has directed my paths and will continue to do so right up to my final day. Such a day will eventually come for us all. Get ready. It will be here before you know it.

At the very end of the C.S. Lewis book *The Last Battle,* some of the characters were discussing the difference between the old Narnia and this new kingdom they were looking to enter ... heaven. Heaven was described as the following:

> *a new...deeper country: every rock and flower and blade of grass looked as if it meant more (and it does). I can't describe it any better than that: if you ever get there you will know what I mean.*

It was the Unicorn (the one Peter had previously ridden into battle) who summed up what everyone was feeling.

---

[97] Charlotte Elliott (lyrics), *Just as I am,* (Public Domain, 1836).

> *"He stamped his right forehoof on the ground and neighed and then cried: 'I have come home at last! This is my real country! I belong here. This is the land I have been looking for all my life, though I never knew it till now.'"*[98]

The adventures in "Narnia" have nearly ended for many of us. What we know is this: People who love "Aslan," the Lion of Judah, the Son of the Most High, the Lamb of God, Jesus, will be with him forever, and that story will have no end. Eternity looms in the distance.

Your story. Your choice. Your adventure. Grow old, yes, but finish strong until the day God calls you home at last.

Here's one more thing. A closing word for those who have yet to finish the last chapter of their own story that has yet to be written. Fear not. The end is coming and coming fast. Before that day arrives, you may be given the opportunity and privilege of interacting with, or caring for older individuals who are nearing the end of their journey. I found the following true story some years ago and never forgot it. Insightful, meaningful, and powerful, worth the read.

In the geriatric ward of a small hospital in North Platte, Nebraska, the life of an old man had come to an end. He died with few earthly possessions. There was nothing left of any significant value. When the hospital staff went through his meager possessions, they found this poem written by the old man. Copies were made and distributed to every nurse in the hospital, and one copy found its way to the Christmas edition of the News Magazine of the St. Louis Association for Mental Health. A little old man, with nothing left to his name, was the author of this challenging poem.

---

[98] C.S. Lewis, *The Last Battle,* (London: United Kingdom, HarperCollins, 2009), 210.

Crabby Old Man

What do you see, nurses? What do you see?
What are you thinking when you're looking at me?
A crabby old man, not very wise,
Uncertain of habit with faraway eyes?

Who dribbles his food and makes no reply.
When you say in a loud voice, "I do wish you'd try!"
Who seems not to notice the things that you do.
And forever is losing a sock or shoe?

Who, resisting or not, lets you do as you will,
With bathing and feeding, the long day to fill?
Is that what you're thinking? Is that what you see?
Then open your eyes, nurse, you're not looking at me.

I'll tell you who I am, as I sit here so still,
As I do at your bidding, as I eat at your will.
I'm a small child of ten with a father and mother,
Brothers and sisters who love one another.

A young boy of sixteen with wings on his feet
Dreaming that soon now, a lover he'll meet.
A groom soon at twenty, my heart gives a leap.
Remembering, the vows that I promised to keep.

At twenty-five, now, I have young of my own.
Who need me to guide, and a secure happy home.
A man of thirty, my young now grown fast,
Bound to each other with ties that should last.

At forty, my young sons have grown and are gone,
But my woman's beside me to see I don't mourn.
At fifty, once more, babies play 'round my knee,
Again, we know children, my loved one and me.

Dark days are upon me. My wife is now dead.
I look at the future. I shudder with dread.
For my young are all rearing young of their own.
And I think of the years ... And the love that I've known.

I'm now an old man, and nature is cruel.
'Tis jest to make old age look like a fool.
The body, it crumbles, grace and vigor depart.
There is now a stone, where I once had a heart.

But inside this old carcass, a young guy still dwells.
And now and again, my battered heart swells.
I remember the joys. I remember the pain.
And I'm loving and living life over again.

I think of the years all too few ... gone too fast.
And accept the stark fact that nothing can last.
So open your eyes people, open and see.
Not a crabby old man. Look closer ... see ... ME!![99]

Finish strong. Finish the race right to the end, making the most of the days you've got left. Live fully and wholeheartedly. Serve Christ with reckless abandon, as best you can, wherever God has placed you. He is worth your finest effort, your best work. Use every resource at your disposal, every ounce of strength you have left, every God-given talent you can muster to advance the kingdom of God and the Good News that Christ, *"while we were yet sinners ... died for us"* (Romans 5:8). Proclaim the name of Jesus and the love and mercy of God, the greatest story ever told, whether healthy or sick, whether you are strapped to a hospital bed or confined to a wheelchair unable to walk. Carry on until the end when *"all hell rejoices that you are out of the fight."*[100] Grow old, yes, but finish strong. Let's get to it …

Remember. This is not your final home. Neither is it mine. There is much, much more to come …

---

[99] Anonymous, Crabby Old Man, Posted by Charles Tutor, *Rotary Club of Highlands Ranch*, Highlands Ranch, Colorado, retrieved from https://rotaryclubhr.org/stories/the-poem-crabby-old-man.
[100] Op.cite, Lewis.

About the Author

Sanford "Sandy" Zensen is an ordained Baptist and former Christian & Missionary Alliance minister with over twenty years of pastoral ministry experience. In addition, he has served for twenty-five years as a professor of Christian studies and as a Christian college administrator. He holds two professional degrees, an MDiv and a DMin, as well as a PhD in religion and society.

Sandy is a frequent speaker at churches, men's ministries, college alumni functions, and athletic events. He was the 2014 AGS (Adult and Graduate Studies) commencement speaker at Bryan College in Tennessee and is the author of seven books. He continues to serve as a member and Sunday school teacher at Stuart Heights Baptist Church, one of the largest Southern Baptist churches in Chattanooga, Tennessee.

OTHER BOOKS BY
Sanford Zensen

On the Wall with Sword and Trowel (WIPF and Stock, 2019)

Living Deep in a Shallow World (WIPF and Stock, 2020)

The Most Important Decision You'll Ever Make (WIPF and Stock, 2021)

The Divine Inquiry, (WIPF and Stock, 2023)

Lord, Why? Questioning God When Life Hurts (WIPF and Stock, 2024)

Living A Life That Matters (WIPF and Stock, 2025)

www.ingramcontent.com/pod-product-compliance
Lightning Source LLC
Chambersburg PA
CBHW070457090426
42735CB00012B/2587